BRADNER LIBRARY
SCHOOLCRAFT COLLEGE
18600 HAGGERTY ROAD
LIVONIA, MICHIGAN 48152

SCHOOLCRAFT COLLEGE LIBRARY

 **W9-BNF-426**

BL 624 .P455 1990

Perrino, Anthony Friess.

One hundred percent half
right

WITHDRAWN

ONE HUNDRED
PERCENT
HALF RIGHT

One Hundred Percent Percent Half Right

THE TRICKY BUSINESS OF SAVING— AND SAVORING—THE WORLD

ANTHONY FRIESS PERRINO

John Daniel and Company
SANTA BARBARA · 1990

Copyright ©1990 by Anthony Friess Perrino
All rights reserved
Printed in the United States of America

Cover design by Francine Rudesill
Design and typography by Jim Cook/Santa Barbara

Published by John Daniel & Company, Publishers, Post Office Box 21922, Santa Barbara, California 93121. John Daniel & Company books are distributed to the trade by National Book Network, 4720 Boston Way, Lanham, Maryland 20706

LIBRARY OF CONGRESS CATALOGING-IN-PUBLICATION DATA
Perrino, Anthony Friess.
   One hundred percent half right : the tricky business of saving and savoring the world / Anthony Friess Perrino.
      p.   cm.
   ISBN 0-936784-84-9: $9.95
   1. Spiritual life—Unitarian Universalist authors. 2. Moral conditions. 3. World politics—1985-1995. I. Title.
BL624.P455   1990   90-31915
248.4—dc 20   CIP

Dedicated to the
First Unitarian Church of Cleveland, Ohio,
with high hopes

One Hundred Percent Half Right

PREFACE:
The Meaning of
the Yin/Yang

THE ANCIENT Chinese religion of Taoism contends that everywhere in nature there is a counter-balancing of opposites. These opposing but complementary forces are designated by the terms Yin and Yang.

At the physical level it is observed that there is hot and cold, light and dark, wet and dry, male and female, and as the song says, "You can't have one without the other."

This wholistic dualism can be seen in other aspects of human experience. Emotionally we feel joy and sorrow, pleasure and pain, love and hate. In the realm of values, we know good and evil, truth and falsehood, beauty and ugliness. In Taoism even the traditional dichotomies of mind and body, idealism and realism, and objectivity and subjectivity are not seen as contradictory but complementary counter-balances to each other: half of the whole truth about life, the Yin and the Yang. The eleventh poem of the *Tao Te Ching* says, "What gives the clay cup its value is the empty space its walls create."

The Yin/Yang symbol is made of two inverted teardrop shapes: one dark and one light which, together, form a full circle. Most representations include a small spot of the other's color inside its opposing half: the implication being that every thought, every feeling, every truth has something of its opposite in it. No idea is pure, none is absolute, none is whole by itself. This reality is also represented by the fact that it is impossible to cut the Yin/Yang circle in half with a straight line without having a part of each "teardrop" in both halves. In Taoist thought, therefore, there is no such thing as 100 percent maleness or femaleness, 100 percent joy or sorrow, pure goodness or pure evil, total truth or total falsehood. Every truth has error in it, every error has some truth in it. For example, a forty-year-old man who says he is thirty-five is expressing a truth: he is afraid of growing old.

In Taoism, all life is seen as a process: the natural flow of things toward balance. As another of its poems says:

> All things bear the Yin on their backs
> and the Yang in their arms.
> By the blending of breath
> from the Yin and the Yang
> equilibrium comes to the world.

We cannot breathe in—unless we also breathe out. We also cannot know joy unless we know sorrow; we cannot say "yes," meaningfully, unless we can say "no."

Taoism presents us with the symbol of Yin/Yang and contends that a wise person will learn to live with the rhythmic flow of the nature of things: an alternating balance of the opposing forces of life.

INTRODUCTION:
The Tricky Business of Saving—and Savoring—the World

TO FEEL a sense of harmonious wholeness within ourselves and with the world around us—that is what everyone desires. As Lillian Smith wrote, "There are two journeys every one of us must make: into our own hearts, accepting what we find there, and into the world, accepting it as our home."

I contend that we must undertake both of these journeys if we are to live whole and healthy lives. And keeping these two crucial concerns in balance is the tricky business of living well.

I focus on this matter because so many people I know seem preoccupied with the inward journey and are prone to what has been described as the new narcissism, or are so committed to social activism that they neglect the inner self. Both fail to maintain the vital balance necessary to living wholly.

11

I became a minister because that profession seemed to offer me the best opportunity to make my life matter—to influence the world around me and thereby gain enduring significance for my days. Like the little boy who described his birth certificate as his "excuse for being born," I wanted to justify my existence on the earth.

I was clearly committed to an activist definition of salvation seeking; I believed that a sense of well-being is earned by doing good work. I fully accepted George Bernard Shaw's contention that "The only true joy in life [is] being used by a purpose recognized by yourself as a mighty one."

The seminary I attended reinforced that belief. Ours was to be a ministry which saw the great social issues of the day as the raw material from which we would fashion our personal salvation. We were taught that "The way to heaven is straight through the heart of a hurting humanity."

With single-hearted devotion, I spent my life in the service of worthy causes—writing, speaking, and marching in Selma, Detroit, Washington, or wherever the action was. I felt that this was what life was all about—using our time on earth to make it into a place of freedom and justice and peace.

At some point I began to wonder if that wasn't 100 percent half right. Perhaps I became disillusioned with the slow rate of change in society, the seeming hopelessness of the task. Perhaps it was a growing awareness that many of my social action co-workers were motivated by an angry need to vent their own unhappiness, rather than a genuine concern for others. Perhaps I was entering a "mid-life passage," when people begin to look inward and give thought to long-neglected personal needs.

Whatever the motivation, I turned my attention toward the inward journey and discovered a self-awareness that does not depend upon external achievement for a sense of well-being. It sees life as more a matter of being than a matter of doing.

Eastern religions and the growth movement psychologies taught me the intrinsic value of simply being myself. Transactional Analysis assured me that I was okay, and demonstrated that a recognition of that fact was the basic requirement of personal growth. Gestalt Therapy helped me get in touch with my feelings and see them as the source of my strength. Indeed, all of the persuasive arguments of the human potential movement convinced me that nurturing self-worth is the only healthy foundation for effecting social change. In short, I came to believe that wholeness is not something to be achieved by mighty striving but is a gift of grace to be gratefully accepted. And morally responsible behavior issues forth naturally from that awareness.

In the words of *The Desiderata*, "You are a child of the universe with an intrinsic right to be here." It is a transforming thought, which clearly contributes to a sense of well being. It is also subtly seductive, another one of life's 100 percent half-right truths.

My personal response to that recognition was not totally to abandon social concerns. I continued to make periodic pronouncements on world hunger, racial injustice, and other causes of human anguish. But I was not feeling the suffering as much, or sacrificing very much to alleviate it.

I would not favor a return to the martyrdom that neglects its own needs for the sake of social progress, but I think there is a narcotic effect which accompanies a preoccupation with self-fulfillment. The fact is that there can be no self-fulfillment apart from caring relationships. We are social beings and need the context of community to be whole selves. There is no sense of wholeness for you or me or anyone unless we are responsibly related to the world around us. That is why self-actualization, as a goal, is self-defeating. It is a case not of either/or but of both/ and, in vital balance.

An obviously literate graffiti writer once wrote on a wall:

> To live is to do.
> —Signed, Sartre.
>
> To live is to be.
> —Signed, Socrates.
>
> Do-Be, Do-Be, Do-Be-Do.
> —Signed, Sinatra.

The balance is more seriously suggested in one of the concepts of Buddhism, "the Bodhisattva"—a person who has attained such personal insight that he or she could enter into complete bliss, but refuses to do so because it would mean forsaking the interconnectedness of life, without which personal fulfillment is meaningless.

E.B. White once posed the problem that all of us face: "I arise each morning with conflicting desires to save and to savor the world. This makes it hard to plan the day." Of course it does. It is a tricky business, but it is the business of living itself.

ETHICAL ISSUES

How Do We Know
What to Believe?

THE CRUCIAL QUESTION OF RELIGION IS not what we believe, but why we believe it. The content of our faith is not nearly as important as the process which produced it. And everyone harbors certain, perhaps unconscious, assumptions regarding how the truth of a matter can be determined.

Even those who argue that it is impossible, really, to know anything, are expressing a theory of knowledge. Their approach is called "radical skepticism," and it is the basis of a philosophy called "nihilism," which literally means "nothing matters" because truth, meaning, and other values are beyond the scope of human knowing.

That's a defensible position; indeed, on bad days it has some

17

appeal. But if the nihilist is consistent, the logical consequence of such belief is silence. And I've always wondered why anyone would take the trouble to argue such a philosophy if nothing matters anyway.

Most of us aren't that skeptical. We seek to discover truth and discern life's meaning or create it, if necessary, by employing four sources of knowledge. They are: external authority (or revelation), sensory perception, rational deduction, and intuition.

The first recognizes that we believe some things simply because people whose judgment we trust tell us they are true. For example, I believe that Plato and Julius Caesar lived. I have no first-hand knowledge of the matter, but accept the testimony of sources I have come to respect. I similarly rely on scientists, newspapers, doctors, and others whose judgment seems knowledgeable. We all rely on such authority more than we realize we do. How do you know whether the universe is expanding or contracting? Whether or not capital punishment deters capital crime? Whether or not we should take a daily dose of vitamins? I submit that your belief on these matters is based upon the testimony of some authority whose expertise you accept.

Another source of knowledge is sensory perception. We know what we can see, hear, touch, taste and smell—what empirical evidence tells us is true. For example, you know that this book exists.

The third source of knowledge, rational deduction, contends that we believe some things not from authority or empirical evidence, but because we deduce them to be true by the use of reason. If two things are equal to a third thing, they are equal to each other. Logic tells us that. Similarly, one thing cannot be in two different places at the same time. Therefore, if you are reading this book, you are not taking a shower.

More immediately relevant, I know that if all this gets too intellectually abstract, you will stop reading.

Finally, we are informed by intuition, an awareness for which we have no authoritative, empirical or rational basis. We all have hunches regarding what is true—insights which are sometimes later verified in experience. Some of these are as sophisticated as Einstein's theory of relativity, which challenged the prevailing opinion of scientific authorities and proved to be a most plausible explanation of reality. Traditional religion has described this "still, small voice within" as the prompting of the Holy Spirit. However it is described, for many it is the basis for deep belief, the source of profound truth. My intuition is that many of you recognize that none of these fundamental sources of knowledge is infallible. It seems obvious (and, of course, I mean obvious to reason, which reveals my predisposition in this matter) that all of the sources of knowledge—authority, perception, logic, and intuition—are subject to error. None of them, therefore, can be relied upon as the sole avenue of insight.

The "authorities" are all human and, therefore, fallible in their judgments, no matter how great their expertise. Although we must often rely on experts when considering a matter beyond our experience, history has taught us that we must subject their pronouncements to verification. That is why I could never accept what I call a pipeline approach to religion, which regards some authority as being above rational scrutiny. A young woman, whose boyfriend said, "Sarah, it's been revealed to me that we should be married," replied, "John, when it's revealed to me, I'll let you know." All revelation must be subject to such personal verification and the test of reason.

That's obviously in order when the matter in question is of great personal significance. If an historian tells me that Napoleon died of a brain tumor, I'm inclined to take his word for it. But if a doctor tells me that I need brain surgery, I want a second opinion no matter how highly I regard his or her competence in the field. Authorities are human and therefore fallible.

By the same token, sensory perception may be distorted and deceiving. Seeing is believing, we are told, but no two people ever see exactly the same thing. Our visual apparatus, from the lens of the eye to the electrochemical reaction in the brain, is affected by our physical condition, our emotional state, and the particular perspective from which we are looking. Similar problems are presented with our other avenues of sensory perception. Water may feel warm to one hand and cold to the other if the hands themselves are of different temperatures. Sensory perception is inescapably subjective and clearly fallible.

Rational deduction is also subject to error because the premises upon which it rests may be false. This was the case with medieval scholars whose logical consistency could not be faulted, but whose conclusions were erroneous because they were based upon false assumptions, such as the belief that the earth was flat.

One of my favorite stories, reflecting the limits of rational deduction, is that of a teacher who wanted to instruct her students regarding the evils of alcohol. She set out two glasses, one filled with water and the other with gin. When she placed a worm in the water, it swam around happily; when she placed it in the gin, it shriveled up and died. The children were then asked what they had learned from the experiment, and a little boy replied, "People with worms should drink gin!" So much for the fallibility of rational deduction.

And intuition, though often valuable in furnishing insight beyond the ken of perception or reason, is so subject to wishful thinking that it is often erroneous. Intuition is most commonly employed in our choices of the people we love. It seems cold and calculating to make those choices on the basis of reason or authority or empirical evidence, but such choices made purely on feelings are invariably wrong, and sometimes disastrous. As someone quipped, "Anyone who gets married on puppy love is doomed to lead a dog's life!"

Thus, because none of the available sources of knowledge is infallible, all of them must be employed to check and balance each other. I call this the coherency test, suggesting that in the final analysis we must judge to be true that which makes for the most cohesive understanding of reality. Regarding each of them as complementary rather than complete, we must strive to fit the insights of the various sources of knowledge into a harmonious whole.

There may be paradoxical dimensions to that awareness: affirmations of what I call 100 percent half-right truths—ideas which are totally valid only when coupled with their opposites to form the whole truth. But there can be no fundamental contradictions in a coherent understanding of reality.

An example of such paradox in my own belief system is reflected in the paired observations: "The unexamined life is not worth living," but "The constantly examined life is like reading recipes instead of eating." Those two opposite insights form the whole truth for me: the Yin and Yang of the matter.

I propose an approach that integrates all of the traditional bases of belief and uses them continually to test each other in a dynamic and ever-unfolding discovery of truth. Most western religions rely primarily upon authority: the Papal pronouncement, the doctrinal creed, the written revelation; "Jesus loves me; this I know, 'cause the Bible tells me so." Most Eastern religions emphasize intuition and mystical awareness: "It's only with the heart that one sees rightly. . . ." The scientific approach relies upon empirical evidence and rational deduction, and thereby neglects realms of awareness beyond their apprehension. I would accept none of these exclusively but ask questions, submitting every claim of truth to a test of coherency. Who says the Bible says? Has the intuition been verified? From what assumptions does the logic proceed? What are the consequences of such belief?

I would make two further observations.

The first recognizes "the egocentric predicament," the fact that, no matter how hard we try, we cannot get outside of or beyond our own experience. This is not to say that there is no objective reality, but simply that our knowledge of it rests upon our experience, which is inescapably subjective.

We are all like the people in the fable, "The Blind Men and the Elephant"; only when we share our individual awareness with each other do we begin to understand the total truth about the reality we experience separately. That is why any emphasis on individual integrity must be tempered by an equal emphasis on the significance of community. Each of us must decide what is true and meaningful for our lives. But we must also recognize that this individual search for understanding is more fruitfully conducted in community with others similarly committed to the search for truth.

The second observation also has to do with commitment. It recognizes that the deeper truth of life is not something "out there" to be apprehended intellectually, but a reality "in here" to be discovered experientially. Life is not a puzzle to be solved, but a profound mystery to be experienced as we grapple with its larger issues.

The final test of belief, therefore, is behavior based upon it. The only meaningful truths are those forged in the crucible of daily living. To put it another way: it is only when we are true to the highest we know that we come to know the highest there is. Indeed, unless we commit ourselves to the living-out of our convictions, we will never know whether they are valid.

Now all of this may be intellectually interesting, but it does not pass the "so-what? test." It's too abstract. I would, therefore, suggest that when we are dealing with the really important issues of life (like "Is it worth living?"), none of the traditional bases of belief are relevant. We cannot resolve that question except by an act of will. We either choose to believe that life is worthwhile, or we don't. There is no empirical evidence, or logical proof, or reliable authority upon which we can base such a belief. And those who affirm a conviction of the worth of life do so because it creates the kind of world in which we wish to live.

So we sometimes simply decide to believe something (for example, "Human beings are basically decent if given half a chance") because the effect of that belief makes life more meaningful and satisfying. As Dag Hammarskjold wrote in "Markings": "You dare your 'yes' and experience a meaning; you repeat your 'yes' and all things begin to acquire meaning."

Why Do
Good People
Do Bad Things?

A FEW YEARS AGO I DROVE ACROSS GER-
many. I was impressed with many things, one of them being
the autobahn where cars were required to maintain a speed of
eighty miles an hour or stay to the right, in the "slow" lane. I
also marveled at the cultural richness of the country. In Leipzig,
I visited the church where Johann Sebastian Bach had been
choirmaster and the tavern where Goethe had written *Dr.
Faust*. In the countryside I was struck by the lush green
loveliness of the land, and the fact that every picturesque town
was dominated by the tall spire of a church proclaiming the

piety of its people. And I wondered, how could the good citizens of this land produce, or at least passively permit, the terrible evil of Nazism? It then occurred to me that what happened in Germany can be instructive if we recognize its larger implications.

The larger question is "Why do good people sometimes do bad things?" By good people I mean, of course, people like you and me—decent human beings who would not intentionally do evil. By bad things I simply mean actions that are destructive of others, or being passively supportive of such behavior. If you need an example closer to home, think of all the good people in the United States who carried on or condoned the evil of slavery.

Why do basically good people do such bad things? Sometimes we do it thoughtlessly out of ignorance. We acquiesce to atrocity because we are unaware of the suffering being caused. Someone once wrote, "Wars go on because there is no way one person can feel, in his or her own body, the pain which another person experiences." I think that's true, and I'd like to believe that the good people of the United States would be horrified if they could feel the terrible consequences of our government's funding of the Contras in Nicaragua. Innocent men, women and children have been maimed by land mines and killed by weapons made in America and paid for with our taxes.

At a deeper level, bad behavior exhibits an ignorance of the interconnectedness of the human family and the fact that, when we deny the humanity of another, we diminish ourselves. I found a clue to the German capacity for tolerating genocide when I visited the beautiful town of Rothenburg. In St. Jacob's Church there, a famous woodcarving of "The Last Supper" is displayed. Its fascination stems from the fact that all of the figures are made from one piece of wood—except that of Judas. The betrayer of Jesus is carved out of different wood to represent the thought that he does not belong in the human family.

Demagogues have always exploited that kind of thinking to justify their barbarism. Hitler, by characterizing the Jews as "Christ-killers" and a different breed of people, was able to do terrible things to them with the passive acceptance of the "good people" of Germany. But the reality is that the fragile fabric of humanity is a seamless cloth. We are inextricably bound to one another, and every war is a civil war. Good people do bad things when they forget that fact.

An old Hasidic story tells of a rabbi who asked his students how one could recognize the time when night ends and day begins. "Is it when, from a great distance, you can tell a dog from a sheep?" one student asked. "No," said the rabbi. "Is it when, from a great distance, you can tell a date palm from a fig tree?" another student asked. "No," said the rabbi. "Then when is it?" the students asked. "It is when you look into the face of any human creature and see your brother or your sister there. Until then, night is still with us."

Good people also do bad things when they are fearful, hurting, and unhappy. There's a story about a man who was bitten by a rabid dog. By the time the doctor arrived he was busily writing on a piece of paper. "No need to write your will," the doctor said, "we'll pull you through." "This is not my will," the man replied. "It's a list of the people I'm going to bite!" A more serious example is found in a film on the life of the French painter Gauguin. The emotionally tortured artist says with a wry smile, "Life being what it is, we dream of revenge." That is sadly true of many human beings. We have all known people who are bundles of frustration and hurt, looking for a place to vent their pent-up anger.

The most powerfully insightful writing on this subject is contained in a book by a German psychologist, Alice Miller. It's entitled *For Your Own Good* and it recounts the child-rearing practices in her country. She believes they made Hitler's rise to power possible and his subsequent actions tolerable.

In the opening chapter Dr. Miller quotes several German educators, including a Dr. Schreber who, in 1858, gave this typical advice to parents: "The little ones' displays of temper as indicated by screaming or crying without cause should be regarded as the first test of your spiritual and pedagogical principles. Once you have established that nothing is really wrong . . . that the screaming is nothing more than an outburst of temper, the first appearance of willfulness, you should no longer simply wait for it to pass but should proceed in a somewhat more positive way: by stern words, threatening gestures, rapping on the bed or, if none of this helps, by appropriately mild corporal admonitions. . . ." He later adds, "This procedure will be necessary only once or at most twice, and then you will be master of the child forever. . . . A glance, a word, a single threatening gesture will be sufficient to control the child."

Dr. Miller observes that this approach does produce obedient children, but "If there is absolutely no possibility of reacting appropriately to hurt, humiliation, and coercion, then these experiences cannot be integrated into the personality; the feelings they evoke are repressed, and the need to articulate them remains unsatisfied."

After describing some other examples of this philosophy of child rearing, Dr. Miller then summarizes the "false information" which is passed from generation to generation by such "poisonous pedagogy." She lists, among others, beliefs that: obedience makes a child strong; a high degree of self-esteem is harmful; severity and coldness are a good preparation for life; parents are always right.

Is it any wonder that children so reared grow up into good people capable of doing bad things? Rollo May wrote, "Violence is a symptom. The disease is powerlessness, insignificance, injustice—in short, a conviction that I am less than human, and I am homeless in the world." And, as Dr. Miller observes, "The easier it becomes, by means of technology, to destroy human life with the touch of a button, the more important it is [that we] understand how it can be possible for someone to want to extinguish the lives of millions of human beings."

Good people do bad things because they are fearful, hurting, and unhappy, unconsciously needing a way to express their rage.

Finally, there is a more subtle reason that good people sometimes do bad things. We have suppressed what psychiatrist Carl Jung called "the shadow side" of our personalities, that part of us that is capable of violence and cruelty. This "dark side" is so ugly and frightening that we disown it, usually by projecting it upon others.

D.H. Lawrence once confessed,

> This is what I believe:
> That my soul is a dark forest,
> That my known self will never be
> more than a clearing in the forest,
> That gods, strange gods, come
> forth from the forest
> into the clearing of my known self,
> and then go back,
> That I must have the courage to
> let them come and go.

Most of us refuse to recognize the "strange gods." We seek scapegoats, people upon whom we can fasten our faultiness, who are then seen as so diabolically evil that anything we do to them is justified. The Germans saw the Jews that way. One of the first things that Hitler did when he came into power was to abolish "Busstag," the national day of repentance for the Germans' launching of World War I. That act marked the beginning of the nation's descent into barbarism.

Americans are capable of the same mentality. We think of ourselves as a morally righteous nation, but our national identity began by stealing this land from the Native Americans and branding them as savages to justify the plunder. More recently in Vietnam and Central America, by projecting our capacity for evil on the specter of Communism, our nation has caused still more suffering.

My purpose is not to depict the United States as inhumanly evil. We are all too human in this capacity. We simply need to acknowledge it, instead of seeking scapegoats upon whom we can project our shadow side. The film *Blue Velvet* sought to confront American viewers with this dark side of human character. It is ugly and terrifying, and most people found the movie too distasteful to be instructive. But the fact is that good people do bad things when we fail to acknowledge that capacity for destructive behavior.

How shall we overcome these sources of bad behavior?

We can deal with the ignorance by seeking a greater awareness of the consequences of our acts and a deeper sense of the interconnectedness of the human family.

We can deal with the fear and pain by recognizing that hurt begets hurt and hate begets more hate. And the only way the vicious cycle is stopped is when someone demonstrates the strength to love.

And we can banish "the shadow" by bringing the light of honesty into our self-consciousness and admitting our capacity for sin and our need for forgiveness.

What Makes a
Nation Great?

Wの HEN THE PILGRIMS CAME TO THIS
land 470 years ago, their pastor aboard the *Mayflower* read
from the Book of Genesis: "And I will make you a great nation
and you will be a great blessing to all mankind." Every American wants to believe that this was prophetic, that America has
become a great nation and a blessing to all humankind. But if
ours is to be an honest pride and a thoughtful patriotism, we
must measure the stature of our nation against legitimate
standards of greatness.

What makes a nation truly great? I would suggest that it is
not the size of the country or its wealth or its power. To
describe a nation as great is to make a value judgment which

has more to do with strength of character than physical might, more to do with richness of culture than material prosperity, more to do with greatness of spirit than vastness of territory.

What makes a nation great and deserving of our devotion are the ideals for which it stands, the values it serves.

A great nation is one which is intellectually free, which allows a diversity of opinion to detect and correct its errors. It provides its citizens with an atmosphere which fosters creativity and nurtures growth. It recognizes that freedom is as essential to the health of a nation as air to breathe.

A great nation is also one which is morally just, maintaining laws which protect the rights of all its citizens. It provides programs which promote social and economic justice: education for the young, security for the old, and equal opportunity for all. It regards the preservation of the rights of its people as its purpose for existence.

And a great nation is one which is a responsible member of the world community, one which uses its power and wealth to serve humankind. History is strewn with wreckage of once-mighty empires. Those nations which are not mindful of the interdependence of all people are not only not great, they are doomed to disaster.

Using these criteria, let us measure the stature of our own nation.

On the test of freedom our record is generally good. We have had our dark periods, when demagogues like Joe McCarthy were able to exploit the fears of the people and convince them that certain political views ought not to be allowed, but such men and moods have not lasted long in our national history. Thanks to the vigilance of organizations like the American Civil Liberties Union and the diligence of the Supreme Court in upholding the Bill of Rights, dissenters have been able to express unpopular opinions without fear of imprisonment.

But this freedom must be regularly reasserted if it is to survive. It wasn't long ago that criticism of our nation's intervention in the Vietnam war was designated as disloyalty by no less a public figure than the President of the United States. But that demagoguery was repudiated by mounting numbers of protest marchers and a free press.

Therein lies my concern about a continuation of the freedom which has made our nation great. People must ever uphold and exercise the right of free expression, or it will be lost. To paraphrase Mark Twain, "Those who don't exercise their freedom of expression have no advantage over those who are not free." And those who would stifle freedom in the name of security must be told that to do so is, eventually, to lose both.

The American historian Henry Steele Commager once wrote: "We do not need to fear ideas but the censorship of ideas. We do not need to fear criticism but the silencing of criticism. We do not need to fear resistance to political leaders but un-questioning acquiescence in whatever policies those leaders adopt." I agree. The only way to know when the government is wrong, to correct it and keep it strong, is to keep it intellectually free.

Regarding the ideal of justice for all, our national record is less admirable. We have made some gains in recent years, but the history of our treatment of Native Americans, of Black people, of the poor among us, and of women generally, has not lived up to our human rights rhetoric.

Dick Gregory once said, "I wouldn't mind paying my income tax if I knew the money was going to a friendly country." Black people have particular reason to wonder about the American promise of "justice for all." And recently we have had a government in Washington which justified its benign neglect of the needy by contending that welfare programs "discourage individual initiative." The same administration, however, was not averse to subsidizing wealthy tobacco farmers, nor reluctant to write blank checks to the profiteers of weaponry whose record of waste is a national disgrace.

If we continue to pour billions of dollars into armaments while our large cities rot, we'll soon have the best protected slums in the world. No one will have to attack us; the nation will collapse from internal decay. Unless our nation begins to devote as much energy to the securing of economic justice as it does to military might, we cannot describe ourselves as a great nation.

On the matter of responsibility among the nations of the world, we would again get mixed reviews from any objective observer. America has done many humanitarian things over the years, but we have also been outrageously immoral on occasion. We have been so, of course, as nations are, to serve our own economic interests. When Major General Smedley Butler retired in 1935, he described this seamy side of our history with these words: "I spent thirty-three years in active military service as a member of . . . the Marine Corps. . . . And during that period I spent most of my time being a high-class muscle man for big business, for Wall Street and for the bankers. . . . I helped make Mexico and especially Tampico safe for American oil interests in 1914. I helped make Haiti and Cuba a decent place for the national City Bank to collect revenues. I helped in the raping of half a dozen Central American republics for the benefit of Wall Street. I helped purify Nicaragua for the international banking house of Brown Brothers in 1909-12. I brought light to the Dominican Republic for American sugar interests in 1916. In China in 1927 I helped see to it that Standard Oil went its way unmolested. During those years, I had, as the boys in the back room would say, a swell racket. I was rewarded with honors, medals and promotion. Looking back on it, I feel that I might have given Al Capone a few hints.

The best he could do was to operate his racket in three city districts. I operated on three continents!"

If you are inclined to write off those words as the raving of one confused military man, I would point out that when General David Schoup, the Marine Corps Commandant, retired during the Vietnam war, he had similar things to say about that conflict: "I believe that if we would have kept our dirty, bloody, dollar-crooked fingers out of the business of these nations so full of depressed, exploited people, they would arrive at a solution to their problems."

Fueled by a fanatic fear of Communism, we are engaged in an arms race that threatens to destroy the whole human family. For some reason, the retired military men seem to be most aware of the madness of it. President Dwight D. Eisenhower said in 1959: "We pay for a single fighter plane with a half billion bushels of wheat. We pay for a single destroyer with new homes that could have housed more than eight thousand people. Is there no other way the world can live?"

There is another way for the world to live, and if America is to lay claim to being a great nation, we will pioneer the path toward disarmament and the creation of an interdependent humanity.

During the celebration of our nation's bicentennial, Henry Steele Commager wrote a "Declaration of Interdependence" based on our own Declaration of Independence. It said, "When in the course of history the threat of extinction confronts mankind, it is necessary for the people of the United States to declare their interdependence with the people of all nations and to embrace those principles and build those institutions which will enable mankind to survive and civilization to flourish."

If the President of the United States would go before the United Nations with such a proclamation, he would be demonstrating the character of a great nation. He will do that, however, only if the people of this land rise up and demand such leadership. Carl Sagan recently expressed the urgency of the need: "What a waste it would be, after four billion tortuous years of evolution, if the dominant organism on earth contrived its own self-destruction."

However severe my criticism in this assessment of the greatness of America, mine is a lover's quarrel with my native land. With all her faults, I see no other nation that holds more hope for humanity or lays a greater claim on my allegiance. We have a heritage of noble ideals and, I think, the capacity to live up to them. My faith was expressed by Thomas Wolfe: "I think the true discovery of America is before us. I think the true fulfillment of our mighty and immortal land is yet to come. And that this glorious assurance is not only our living hope, but our dream to be accomplished. . . ."

Freedom's
Holy Light

IF "LOVE" IS THE MOST MALIGNED AND
misused word in the English language, and I think it is, the next
candidate for that dubious distinction is "freedom." It is a word
which we learn to pronounce with reverence, and rightly so, for
liberty is a priceless possession. But how carelessly we use the
term. For some, to be free merely means to be unbuttoned; it is
equated with license. And "free enterprise" is often a euphemism for the right to exploit others without governmental
interference.

In the realm of international politics, we talk of "the free
world" and mean those nations which are aligned with our

foreign policy, a designation which has historically included such dictatorships as that of Franco's Spain, Salazar's Portugal, and Somoza's Nicaragua.

There are many facets to the concept of freedom. I will explore its political significance in the context of a statement made by Jean Jaures, the French political philosopher: "Take from the altars of the past the fire, not the ashes!" That is a crucial insight. It's obvious and yet neglected. We must take from the altars of our nation's past the living fire of freedom, rather than the ashen residue of its flame. And in order to do that we must learn to distinguish the fire from the ashes.

Several years ago, when U.S. troops were sent to Cyprus to help the British put down a rebellion there, some of the soldiers decided to celebrate the Fourth of July with fireworks. Villagers, hearing the noise, came running out of their homes to see what was causing the commotion. An army sergeant explained that they were commemorating America's Independence Day. One of the townspeople asked with a sly smile, "Independence from whom?" The sergeant replied sheepishly, "Oh, well, that was a long time ago."

More recently, in Madison, Wisconsin, a newspaper reporter stood on a street corner and asked people to sign an unidentified copy of the Declaration of Independence. Some said it sounded "too radical," others branded it "subversive" and "un-American," and none of the sixty-seven people who were asked would affix their names to this basic document of our democracy. Similar experiments elsewhere have yielded similar responses.

If we would sing "Long may our land be bright with freedom's holy light" and mean it, if we would take the flame of freedom from the altars of the past and "secure the blessings of liberty for ourselves and our posterity," we had better learn to distinguish the fire from the ashes.

Equally important is the fact that, if we are to take the fire from the altars of the past, we must risk getting burned occasionally. Just as fire can be dangerous, freedom can be abused; it does not always work to our immediate advantage. That is why there are some who prefer benevolent tyranny. George Bernard Shaw once said that he "so passionately wanted efficient government of the people and for the people, he could never accept government by the people."

It's true that striving to preserve the flame of freedom carries the risk of being burned, by inefficiency or worse. There will be those who use their freedom to deceive and mislead, and there will be the possibility of traitors hiding behind constitutional guarantees of rights. These risks are inherent in a free society, but it's better to take the calculated risk than to accept the certain alternative of tyranny. Better to be singed by the fire of freedom than suffocated in the ashes of authoritarianism. If we have faith in the people's capacity ultimately to recognize truth, we will know that the only enduring political security is to be found where a free exchange of opinions is maintained. Thomas Jefferson wrote: "In a democracy, error by the majority may be tolerated as long as the minority is free to correct it." This is its genius and strength.

Dictatorships are doomed to failure because no one dares criticize their error. So freedom does function like a refining fire, consuming falsehood and revealing truth. That is why it is so ironic that the self-designated super patriots, in the name of loyalty, would suppress freedom for dissent. It is what has made, and would keep, our nation strong. For that reason it is stupid, as well as un-American, to say, "My country right or wrong." A democratic society depends upon its critics to correct its mistakes.

The greatest danger to our nation was illustrated in a Herblock cartoon which depicted a man labeled "Hysteria" running up a ladder to the torch held by the Statue of Liberty. He is carrying a bucket of water and hollering "Fire!"

Years ago the rising waters behind one of the great dams in the Tennessee Valley were threatening to engulf an old log cabin. A new home had been built for the family on a location safely above the high water mark, but the people refused to move. Their resistance was related to the fire on the hearth of the cabin. "My grandpa built that fire a hundred years ago," the man explained. "He never let it go out for he had no matches, and it was a long trip to the neighbor's. When Grandpa died, my pa tended that fire and since he died, I've tended it. None of us ever let it die, and I ain't gonna move away and let Grandpa's fire go out." The engineers brought a large iron kettle, gathered up the coals in the old fireplace, and carried them to the new house, where fresh kindling was added. And the family was able to move from their cabin in the valley to the new home on the hill and take with them the fire of their ancestors.

The story aptly reveals that if we would carry the flame of freedom into a new generation, a container is necessary. We need a context for the fire. In short, there is no freedom apart from responsibility; no liberty without community. For freedom to thrive requires a framework of recognized obligations.

That is why the Constitution, aptly described as a "Declaration of Interdependence," had to follow the Declaration of Independence—to furnish a context of law in which our freedom could function. Listen to its Preamble: "We the people of the United States, in order to form a more perfect union, establish justice, insure domestic tranquillity, and secure the blessings of liberty for ourselves and our posterity do ordain and establish this Constitution." Someone once suggested that we ought to have a Statue of Responsibility on the West Coast to balance the Statue of Liberty on the East Coast and remind us of the context of our freedom. It is a worthy thought.

The song "America" wisely includes the words "confirm thy soul in self-control, thy liberty in law" because whenever people do not exercise their freedom responsibly, they invite the curtailment of that liberty. Cries of outrage at "government interferences with private enterprise" fail to recognize that, if farmers were treating migrant workers fairly, there would be no need for laws to protect the workers; if Blacks weren't being discriminated against, there would be no need for civil rights legislation; if landlords weren't behaving irresponsibly, there would be no need for rent control.

As Edmund Burke wrote two hundred years ago, "[We] are qualified for civil liberty in exact proportion to [our] disposition to put moral chains on [our] own appetites. [People] of intemperate minds cannot be free; their passions forge their fetters." Carrying the flame of freedom from the altars of our past requires a context of responsibility, which if not self-imposed will be imposed by government.

But there was a second element in the story of "Grandpa's fire." After the coals were carried to the new fireplace, "fresh kindling was added to the fire," which is to say that if we are to keep alive the flame of freedom from the altars of the past, we must continually replenish it.

"New occasions teach new duties," James Russell Lowell wrote, observing that freedom must be reinterpreted and renewed by every generation. Like anything else alive, it must be constantly growing to be relevant for changing times. That is why "the apprenticeship of liberty is unending." It is the requirement of a free society's survival that each generation rediscover this truth.

The Ancient Roots
of Homophobia

I N 1973 THE AMERICAN PSYCHIATRIC ASSO-
ciation voted to remove homosexuality from the classification
of mental disorders. In doing so, the doctors recognized that just
because the particular homosexuals who came to see them were
disturbed about their sexual orientation did not mean that all
homosexuals were neurotic. Being gay, as lesbians and male
homosexuals prefer to be called, is itself no longer seen as an
illness by the medical profession.

But many persons in our society still view the homosexual
act as unnatural and immoral, "a sin against God and man." In
most states it is illegal, and in one state the penalty for sexual

acts between consenting adults of the same sex is greater than that imposed upon a convicted rapist or child molester.

In North Carolina, an 1837 law based on a 1533 British statute reads: "Any person who shall commit the abominable and detestable crime against nature, not to be mentioned among Christians . . . shall be adjudged guilty of a felony and shall suffer death, without benefit of clergy." As it stands today, the death penalty is omitted but a sixty-year sentence is prescribed, and one man is currently serving a thirty-year term for a single homosexual act with a consenting adult.

The slang term "fag" is derived from the word faggot, which the dictionary defines as "a bundle of sticks used as fuel for fire." The term refers to the historical fact that homosexuals were once burned at the stake. Today we are more sophisticated in our cruelty toward those who differ from the majority of us, but similarly inhumane. We brand as dangerous outcasts and ostracize those so predisposed. As a Vietnam veteran put it, "The government gave me medals for killing many men and gave me a dishonorable discharge for loving one."

How did we come by such emotionally-charged attitudes and vengeful behavior toward those whose only crime is that of being different sexually? I think the roots of our feelings are embedded in two ancient religious beliefs.

The first stems from primitive religious rites designed to placate the wrath of powerful and fickle deities. In the beginning these rituals consisted of various activities performed to please the gods and cultivate their good will: the burning of incense, pouring libations of perfumed oil (the aroma ascending and giving pleasure), a variety of animal sacrifices, and so forth. Then there developed what are called rites of aversion, practices designed to disarm the malevolence of the deities by bringing pain upon yourself. This would make the gods feel sorry for you and less malevolent. Fasting, mortification of the flesh, and various kinds of self-inflicted suffering became sacred ritual.

This latter category of religious activity engendered taboos regarding physical pleasure, which was thought bad because it would make the gods jealous. It also nurtured the thought that pain was good because it evoked the sympathy of the deities. The notion lingers today in the popular beliefs that any experience of unbridled pleasure will cost you ("Play on Monday, pay on Sunday"), and that "suffering is good for the soul."

If you accept the idea that what feels good must be bad, sexual pleasure, which is one of the greatest physical pleasures a human being can experience, is particularly evil.

The early Christians assimilated this taboo in their view that "All sex hath somewhat of sin in it." (St. Jerome, in the fourth century, suggested that a man who loves even his own wife too ardently is guilty of sin.) Understandably, the Church Fathers wanted their adherents to be devoted to the spiritual rewards of the next world, and such devotion would be undermined by too much pleasure in this one. The term for all this is asceticism, and it took many forms— withdrawal into monasticism with its avoidance of worldly delights, the self-inflicted torture of the hair shirt, and celibacy for those who chose the religious vocation and desired to maintain their purity.

The second source of our culture's attitudes toward sexuality is rooted in Hebrew history. The Jews were a small tribe of people living a precarious existence. Surrounded by hostile forces and an environment which threatened their extinction, they had to "be fruitful and multiply," as their scripture put it, if they were to survive as a race. This emphasis upon procreation carried with it a corresponding condemnation of any enjoyment of the pleasure which did not produce children. Onan's "spilling his seed upon the ground" was regarded as sinful because he wasted the precious substance upon which the survival of the

Jewish people depended. Because the ancient Jews felt a sacred obligation to beget children, they came to regard as sinful any sexual activity that did not produce offspring. That is why, in 1000 B.C., homosexuality came to be regarded as an "abomination."

In the Greek and Roman culture, however, there was no need for such an emphasis, and the people were able to regard sexual pleasure as a legitimate end in itself. Homosexuality was openly practiced and accepted.

Today we no longer have a need to be fruitful and multiply. What is needed is the curtailment of population growth. But, as often happens, those ancient environmental circumstances produced beliefs which we later designated as divine injunction. We are now governed by patterns of presumed "natural law," as though they were delivered from on high by God in King James English.

The same Book of Leviticus which contains the Biblical condemnation of homosexuality as an abomination also includes a similar proscription against the eating of rabbit and shellfish. But few people regard the consumption of clams as the violation of sacred law. Similarly, the New Testament Letters of Paul, which condemn homosexuality as sin, also decree that women should be silent in church, a pronouncement which is equally and justifiably ignored.

It is clear that we have inherited a homophobia, a fear of homosexuality which sees it as the sin of enjoying the pleasure of sex without the justification of propagation. Compounding our anxieties about homosexuals is a subconscious awareness of our own capacities for such activity, and that, I think, is the source of the disproportionate hostility we visit upon those so oriented.

Our exaggerated fear about the possibility of our children encountering homosexuals is particularly ludicrous in view of the fact that 98 percent of all child molesters are heterosexual, married males. Add to that fact the psychological reality that most homosexuals are produced, prior to school age, in the homes of heterosexual parents, and the proposed discrimination against teachers who are homosexual is clearly unwarranted.

Arthur Janov, in *The Primal Revolution*, comments on the sexuality issue with which we should be more concerned:

> Just because a person acts out feelings in heterosexual ways rather than in homosexual ones doesn't make him any more healthy. If he is acting out, trying to get the warmth of a parent symbolically through sex, he is still neurotic. Society happens to approve of heterosexual "macho" behavior, so we tend not to see it for sickness. Unfortunately, if he acts out of need for a parent of the same sex, he can be put in jail; if he acts out the need for a parent of the opposite sex, he can be a hero.

There is implicit in that statement a disputable assumption regarding the origins of homosexuality. There is a great deal of debate on this question with experts agreeing that no one really knows how same-sex preference is produced. There is a growing consensus that homosexuals are born, that it is a physiological condition. Some studies have indicated that stress experienced by the mother during pregnancy can cause a hormonal change in the embryonic life. Others insist that homosexuality is the result of psycho-social experiences, particularly the absence of love from the parent of the same sex.

Janov summarizes the last view:

> What is a homosexual? It is a person who has sex with

members of his own gender; or at least wants to. The reasons are diverse. In the case of males it can be a repressed need for father love or a fear of mother (and then women). In the case of females, it can be due to never having a warm mother, or avoidance of men due to fear of incestuous feelings toward father (and later men).

Some psychiatrists share this view, which makes ironic tragedy of the fact that for years fathers were reluctant to show physical affection to their sons, lest the boy grow up to be homosexual. Now it seems that such coldness may be a cause of male homosexuality. Perhaps the most significant thing to say about our present understanding is that there are many kinds of homosexuality, and their origins vary. A more relevant question, upon which scientists tend to agree, is whether or not a homosexual's orientation can be changed.

Dr. Irving Bieber, a New York psychiatrist, claims the most successful effort in that undertaking, and even this success is very limited: after three years of intensive therapy, one-third of his 106 homosexual patients became heterosexual; a few others became bisexual. Many questions arise as a result of Dr. Bieber's work. His patients wanted to change. What of those who are not so motivated? And what about the 60 percent of those treated who wished to change and were unsuccessful, even with Dr. Bieber's help? And, finally, what about the homosexual who cannot afford three years of intensive therapy?

The crucial issue is how shall we relate to those people whose orientation will remain, for whatever reason, homosexual?

Statistical estimates vary, but even conservative judgments suggest that more than five percent of the male population and two percent of the female population have a same-sex preference. Included among them are football players and writers, truck drivers and artists, doctors and lawyers, clergy and teachers, millions of Americans whose appearance and manner is no different from yours and mine.

It has been said that "Love is the capacity to view statistics with compassion." I add the suggestion that if one of those people were your son or daughter, a brother or sister, mother or father, you would not want that person to be subjected to harassment and job discrimination, or denied the nurture of physical affection. We should relate to the homosexual, then, as a human being whose life is of worth, and whose welfare commands our concern.

I also suggest that we should apply the same criteria for evaluating the sexual behavior of a heterosexual to the activities of a homosexual. The only valid basis for judging any act as right or wrong is "How does it affect the lives of those involved?" That which harms human beings is evil; that which enhances human welfare is good. If a sexual act is exploitive, disregarding the worth of another, it is morally wrong, whether heterosexual or homosexual. If, on the other hand, a sexual act between consenting adults is an expression of genuine affection and is mutually enhancing, I cannot regard it as anything but good. To deprive persons of the fulfilling experience of physical love, because their sexual preference is different, is a sin against human nature, a sin against life.

The experience of the homosexual can be better understood if those of us who are left-handed were to consider the possibility of our difference being regarded as a terrible sin. Even though our left-handedness did no one any harm, and try as we might we could not change it, what if, because some ancient writing had branded the trait as "an abomination to the Lord," we were treated with fear and loathing? The analogy, I submit, is an apt one.

It is past time that we set aside the Dark Ages attitude on

this matter. We no longer regard the physically handicapped with fear and brutality. We no longer condone slavery with notions of racial superiority. We no longer imprison eccentrics, who harm no one by their curious behavior. Why in the name of humanity should we brand as immoral those whose only desire is to enjoy the pleasure and emotional nurture of physical love?

Let us be more rational and caring in our response to homosexuality. Let us recognize that there is little enough of the love which nurtures selfhood in our society and be done with the ancient blight of homophobia.

Civil Disobedience in Historical Perspective

I N 1962 PRESIDENT KENNEDY, AT THE SUGgestion of the American Bar Association, proclaimed May 1 as "Law Day, U.S.A." It was intended to counteract the May Day celebrations of Communist nations. The attorney group also sought to enlist the support of the clergy in the observance, sending us a booklet entitled "Religion and the Law."

It was a reasonable enough request. The significance of law as the context of freedom is undeniable. But if Law Day is truly to contrast our approach to that of totalitarian states, the emphasis should be placed on the attitude toward dissent—which makes our philosophies of law different.

The fact is that any nation, particularly a dictatorial one, would urge its citizens to obey the law. The Bar Association booklet could have been used, with minor revisions, anywhere in the world. Particularly illustrative of this fact is the critical attitude it took toward civil disobedience. So I would like to define, defend, and give historical perspective to this much-maligned expression of dissent.

Civil disobedience is an act of breaking the law, not merely a demonstration of protest. I stress this because there are many who regard any expression of public protest as an act of civil disobedience. They forget that "the law of our land" provides for peaceful demonstration as a constitutional right. No matter how tumultuous a demonstration may get, it is not civil disobedience unless the law is broken.

Civil disobedience is also a public act. It is not simply a violation of the law; it is a protest, perpetrated openly, with a willingness to accept the penalty of the law in order to call attention to injustice. The term should not be used to describe cowardly and clandestine acts. Many newspapers fail to make this distinction, identifying criminal acts such as vandalism and looting as civil disobedience. That is irresponsible journalism. There is a vast difference, for example, between draft-card burning and draft dodging. The students who protested the Vietnam war by burning their draft cards were surrendering their "dodge" in order to call attention to what they believed to be an unjust war. Their willingness to go to jail for that act made it truly an act of civil disobedience.

As traditionally practiced, civil disobedience also maintains non-violence. There are times when those engaged in dissent have been driven to violence, in self-defense, but the great examples of the tactic, like Gandhi and Martin Luther King, insisted on employing non-violent means.

An examination of the history of this matter reveals that each age tends to view the civilly disobedient of its own time as "kooks," while regarding those of previous eras as the heroes and heroines of humankind. We build monuments to the prophets of the past, and save the leftover stones to throw at the prophets of the present.

For example, we regard Socrates as the father of academic freedom because he refused to obey the law of Athens, which would have abridged his freedom of speech. He chose instead to accept the consequence of his civil disobedience, in that instance the irrevocable consequence of drinking a hemlock cocktail.

The martyrs of early Christendom were tortured and killed by the thousands because they refused to acknowledge Rome and the emperor as the ultimate authority in their lives. They were willing to "render unto Caesar that which was Caesar's" but not that which belonged to their God, their moral conscience. Later, the champions of religious freedom, people like Michael Servetus, were burned at the stake for refusing to obey the civil law which required their conforming to an orthodox faith. Had they not stood firm in their protests of such laws, had not someone, sometime, somewhere been willing to suffer the cause of religious freedom, you and I would not enjoy it today.

Indeed, our national identity was founded on acts of civil disobedience against legally constituted authority. The rationale for the American Revolution was articulated in the Declaration of Independence. People have certain inalienable rights to life, liberty and the pursuit of happiness . . . and whenever government becomes destructive of those ends, it is the right of the people to alter or abolish it.

But of all the historical events bearing upon the subject, the most significant were the Nuremburg Trials of 1945-46. The defense of the Nazis tried for their atrocities during World War II was that they were only obeying their government, that the law of their land required obedience to their superiors.

The court rejected that defense, arguing that human beings

have a greater moral duty to disobey such monstrous orders. The defendants were convicted because they refused to practice civil disobedience. And our nation proclaimed to the world the belief that there are higher laws than those of the state, laws of decency to which people must give their ultimate allegiance or be held accountable.

My assumption is that you agree with the principle of civil disobedience, and would practice it if faced with a flagrant enough example of injustice and the absence of legal means to correct it. I assume that you believe as I do in the sacredness of individual conscience. Thoreau put it this way: "If we resign our conscience to the legislator, why then have a conscience?" So the issue becomes a matter of degree of dissatisfaction with the injustices which prevail . . . and/or our capacity for accepting the penalties for such radical expression of dissent.

Because civil disobedience requires courage, most of us have a high threshold of pain when it comes to pricking our social consciences. We tolerate terrible injustices, especially when they are visited upon someone else, rather than incur the wrath of the keepers of the status quo.

This is understandable, if not excusable, but we then try to rationalize our passivity by speaking in hallowed terms about respect for the law, as though that were the basis for our reluctance to challenge the injustice. We betray that rationalization, of course, with our casual disobedience of laws which are just and necessary, like traffic regulations, which we violate with impunity. It is inconsistent, if not hypocritical, to obey unjust laws on the grounds that the law is sacred and then disobey reasonable laws because they are personally inconvenient.

To those who fear that tolerance of civil disobedience would lead to anarchy, I contend that in accepting the consequences of its violation of the law, civil disobedience is a responsible expression of dissent. Its purpose is not to flout the law but to use it to effect reform—a gesture of genuine respect for the law. Again the best illustration is Socrates. In bringing him to trial, the authorities didn't want his death, only his submission, and to that end made several attempts to strike a bargain with him. While he was in prison awaiting execution, an escape was arranged by some of his friends. But Socrates would have none of it. He explains his refusal with these words: "Consider it this way. Suppose the laws were to come to me, as I was preparing to run away, and were to ask, 'Tell us, Socrates, what have you in your mind to do by trying to escape but to destroy us and the whole state?' "

He refused to avoid the consequences of his act because that would have been disrespectful of the law and destructive of the state. It would also negate the very purpose of his act: to confront the people with a choice—between his vision of the right and that of the state. To make that choice absolutely inescapable, he insisted that the government either change the law, or bring the full force of it upon him. Martin Luther King did the same thing when he looked down the barrel of the Alabama sheriff's gun and said, "Shoot me or stand aside."

Civil disobedience, in accepting the penalty for breaking the law, demonstrates not disrespect but a high regard for its significance. It is a practice which leads not to anarchy but to a refining and strengthening of a nation's legal process. The strong emotional reaction of some people to civil disobedience stems from the fact that it confronts us all with the realization that to obey an unjust law is as surely a moral choice as to disobey it. This occurred in the confrontation which took place when Thoreau was jailed for refusing to pay a war tax. Emerson visited him and asked, "Henry, what are you doing in there?" Thoreau replied, "Ralph, what are you doing out there?" That's the question which acts of civil disobedience pose to us all.

When Black people, after praying and petitioning and exhausting all legal means of seeking their civil rights, began under Martin Luther King to practice nonviolent civil disobedience, they were met with nightsticks and brickbats. It was understandable to me that some of their more militant leaders wanted to burn the country to the ground. If a society does not allow for the practice of civil disobedience as an aboveboard endeavor to have its injustices corrected, it will invite a violent disobedience which has no regard for civil structure—which is, in fact, anarchy.

Reinhold Neibuhr wrote, "Our capacity for justice is what makes democracy possible. Our capacity for injustice is what makes democracy necessary." I would add that it makes the tolerance of civil disobedience both right and wise.

The Ongoing Evolution of Human Rights

W E HAVE GROWN UP IN A SOCIETY
where the inalienable rights to life, liberty and the pursuit of
happiness are taken for granted, if not always granted to
everyone. It is difficult for us to imagine a time when the
concept of human rights was not respected. But the evolution of
this idea, still far from being fully realized, has been a long
hard-fought struggle. In fact, it did not receive world-wide
articulation until the United Nations Declaration of Human
Rights of 1948.

Historically, there have been three types of government in

human affairs. The first was based upon superstition. Ruled by a privileged priest-craft, which claimed a special pipeline to "divine will," this government legislated for the masses and regulated their lives according to what was described as "God's commands." In that society, human beings had no rights—only duties. Theirs was not to question why but to do what they were told or die—by the order of the witchdoctor, high priest, or whomever that society was gullible enough to accept as the divinely-appointed spokesperson. That sort of government lasted as long as that sort of superstition prevailed—which means that in some places it exists even today.

A second type of government was based on power. Physical might was grasped by conquerors, and their reign lasted as long as their power prevailed. In these societies, no one possessed rights—only privileges in proportion to their position in the power structure. For example, in the Roman Empire citizens had certain rights, but not because they were human beings; those rights and privileges derived from a status conferred by the emperor, who held the power.

The same arrangement prevailed in feudal society. People were grouped into classes, each enjoying a different degree of freedom and privilege, protected by the feudal lord. Again their rights were based not on the fact of their humanity but on their preferred position in relation to the possessors of power.

Some governments, in order to extend their rule, later combined these two forms of government—"united fraud to force and set up an idol which they called the divine right of kings," as Thomas Paine described it. "The key of St. Peter," he added, "and the key of the treasury became quartered on one another, and the wondering, cheated multitude worshipped the invention!"

He was speaking of the Holy Roman Empire, of course, in which government by superstition and government by power were wed, and the rights of human beings were subjugated under that alliance. Anyone contending today that the President of the United States, in the interests of national security, can abrogate the laws of the land is advocating the same kind of theocracy.

The third type of government was inaugurated indirectly, when an effort to challenge papal power and establish independent national sovereignty led political philosophers to proclaim the "social contract theory" of government.

The thesis, articulated most eloquently by Rousseau in 1762, is that since no human being has any natural authority over another, government should be based upon a social contract, freely entered into, which creates reciprocal rights and obligations between its citizens. This political philosophy became the platform for advocates of what was termed "The Common Rights of Man." Women were supposedly included in this declaration, but the male chauvinism of the language reflects the fact women were, and still are even in our nation, awaiting full recognition of equal rights.

In 1789 the French Assembly adopted a "Declaration of the Rights of Man" which included these statements, again in the sexist language of that time: "Men are born, and always continue, free and equal in rights." "The end of all political associations is their preservation of the natural and imprescriptible rights of man." This was the first time in history that a government proclaimed the guarantee of human rights. A century earlier the idea had been expressed by a Jewish philosopher, Baruch Spinoza, who wrote:

> The purpose of the State is not to dominate people, nor restrain them by force; rather it is to free human beings from fear that they may live and act with full security, and without injury to themselves or their neighbors. The end of the State, then, is really liberty.

Thus articulated, the third type of government, that of democracy, is one which not only affirms the capacity of people to govern themselves, but also declares that the very purpose of government is to protect and secure the inalienable rights of its citizenry.

One interesting fact is that these ideas, originally enunciated in Europe, didn't take root and finally flower until the great experiment of American democracy. I suggest that this is true because of the theological foundation which Puritan Christianity, arising out of the Hebrew faith, gave to the concept of human rights.

It stressed the absolute sovereignty of God, and the concomitant belief that all human beings must be free from the authority of the state, or any other human institution, so they can be ultimately responsible to God. The founders of America believed that to give moral allegiance to any lesser authority than the Creator of life was to engage in idolatry. Thus, the Bill of Rights was supported as a political means of preserving that freedom to obey God rather than government.

A recognition of the sinful capacity of human nature, derived from Judeo-Christian Puritan theology, prompted the provision of measures that protected human beings from another's inhumanity. Lord Bryce, commenting on the American Constitution, put it this way: "It is the work of men who believed in original sin and were resolved to leave open for transgression no door they could possibly shut. Compare this spirit with the naive optimism of the French in 1789. It is not merely a difference in temperament; it is a difference in fundamental ideas." Because the French failed to erect safeguards against the human capacity for evil, the revolutionary government there became as despotic as its predecessor.

Historically, however, most of the champions of human rights have maintained a pragmatic rather than religious basis for their beliefs. American Puritanism provided a rich soil for the growth of the idea, but political leaders like Thomas Paine, Benjamin Franklin, and Thomas Jefferson guided that growth with arguments in reason, and sought the preservation of individual rights as the only enduringly sound basis of government.

They contended that all human beings have a right to whatever they need to fulfill their potential as persons. These rights are claimed not only because they are necessary to the development of individuals, but also because granting them enhanced the well-being of that society.

For example, every child has a right to an education not simply because that child needs such learning opportunities to be a fulfilled human being, but because the society needs and will benefit from having an educated citizenry. Similarly, the right to freedom of expression must be protected, not only because it is necessary to the individual's growth, but because such a regard for dissent is indispensable to the health and wealth of the nation.

To put it another way, reflecting another assumption undergirding belief in human rights: corresponding to every right to be enjoyed by citizens of a democracy is a responsibility to be accepted—that of guaranteeing those same rights to others. That's why the Declaration of Independence had to be followed by the Constitution, which has been aptly called A Declaration of Interdependence.

Abraham Lincoln phrased it well: "Those who will not grant freedom to others have no right to it themselves, and under a just God, will not long retain it." Societies which ignore that reality will eventually perish from internal decay.

There are some significant implications to all of this.

One is the fact that the administration of justice recognizes that some rights are more fundamental than others, because they are more necessary to the well-being of individuals and the society.

Courts of justice exist to arbitrate conflicting claims of rights, and every legal case is an endeavor to weigh one party's rights against another's. For example, if I were to charge you with assault, I would be contending that your right to swing your arm stops where my nose begins. And I would claim that my right to physical safety supersedes your right to freedom of movement.

The desire for justice decrees that the physical health and safety of individuals is a more basic right than free speech. That is why we cannot cry "Fire!" in a crowded theater and expect to enjoy immunity from prosecution.

By the same token, human rights must always take precedence over property rights. Just as we are not allowed to burn down our own property because that act jeopardizes the lives of others, property owners should not be allowed, if justice is to be served, to charge exorbitant rent, or maintain substandard safety conditions, or engage in racial discrimination, simply because they own the property.

During election campaigns, an oft-quoted slogan promises to "Get the government off people's backs" and let free enterprise reign. I see that statement as usually meaning, "Leave me alone to exploit whomever I can, without government interference." But the fact of history is that if any nation subordinates human rights to property rights, it will not long endure, for it is violating the deeper demands of justice.

In 1987 we witnessed an historic summit meeting between Soviet Premier Mikhail Gorbachev and our president. The arms agreement they produced was hailed by all who yearn for a peaceful planet as a small but significant step in that direction. On the subject of human rights, however, their conversations were far less fruitful. That was inevitable, I think, because the two leaders approached the matter with different assumptions.

Let me suggest the character of that difference by quoting a Latin American student who had studied in the United States and later wrote:

> I heard Americans talk all the time about the freedoms they wanted us to have; no one seemed concerned about the injustices we can no longer bear. I was not a Communist when I went to the U.S., nor am I one today. But I have returned convinced that the Communist is the only one who understands our problems, and, if you Americans continue on the road you are now following, many of my people will turn to Communism in despair.

The Marxist emphasis on the more fundamental human right of economic justice has a great appeal among the poorer nations of the world, where hunger, shelter, and economic exploitation are the overriding issues. When we criticize socialist nations for their lack of freedom of expression and freedom of movement, they can respond by pointing to our homeless and jobless and suggest that the so-called higher freedoms are meaningless to those who are struggling for sheer survival. As Martin Luther King said about the integration of lunch counters in the south, "What good is it to be free to sit at the counter if you can't afford the price of a hamburger?"

However strongly we may disagree with Communist methods for obtaining a society where the masses are fed and clothed and provided with the necessities of health care and housing, we had better understand the attractiveness of the Communist commitment to such basic human rights. If we do not recognize that the right to life itself precedes the rights to liberty and the pursuit of happiness, we will never be able to achieve economic justice in our own country or lasting peace in the world.

The Right to Life—
With Dignity

AN ELDERLY MAN WAS DIAGNOSED AS having a terminal illness. When he learned that the doctors were planning surgery, the man said, "I don't want to die with tubes sticking out all over me. I don't want my children to remember their father that way. I'm old and tired and have seen enough of life. I want to be a man, not a vegetable that someone comes and waters everyday." In spite of his statement, a feeding tube was installed, intravenous injections were given four times a day, and the man was hooked to a respirator. One night, however, he reached over and turned the respirator off. The next morning on the bedside table, a note was found which said simply, "Death is not the enemy, doctor. Inhumanity is."

After many years in the ministry, during which I've seen people similarly forced to continue a life devoid of dignity, I believe it is inhumane to deny someone who is emotionally stable and incurably ill the right to choose prompt, peaceful death.

I begin with an historical review of what has been termed euthanasia, from two Greek words meaning "happy death." A more stark definition is furnished by the ethicist, Dr. Joseph Fletcher, in a book entitled *Morals and Medicine*. It says, "[Euthanasia] is the theory that in certain circumstances, when owing to disease, senility, or the like, a person's life has permanently ceased to be either agreeable or useful, the sufferer should be painlessly killed, either by himself or by another." He used the word "killed" deliberately, lest we minimize the significance of the act.

The ancient Greeks allowed the practice. As cited earlier, Socrates drank the hemlock rather than live in prison, and it was considered an honorable choice. The Romans, particularly the Stoics, believed in a more limited form of euthanasia, as expressed in these words of Seneca: "If one death is accompanied by torture and the other is simple and easy, why not take the latter?"

Early Christianity objected to euthanasia on the grounds that it violated the commandment "Thou shalt not kill," though that didn't seem to affect their attitude toward capital punishment or war. Modern Roman Catholic theologians translate the commandment as "Thou shalt not murder," which opens the question of whether an induced merciful death can truly be considered murder. A noted Catholic thinker of the sixteenth century, Sir Thomas More, once argued for euthanasia with these words: "When anyone is taken with a torturing and lingering pain, so that there is no hope either of cure or ease. . . . Since they are now become a burden to themselves and all about them, and they have really outlived themselves, they should ... choose rather to die since they cannot live but in misery."

In seventeenth-century Brittany, an incurable sufferer could appeal to the parish priest for "The Holy Stone." The family would gather, the patient would be given the Last Rites, and then the oldest relative would lift the heavy Holy Stone directly above the patient's head and let it fall. Perhaps it was the brutality of such methods which led to the legal circumstance that exists today in most western nations. Euthanasia is considered a crime. Again from Dr. Fletcher, "We are, by some strange habit of mind and heart, willing to impose death but unwilling to permit it: we will justify humanly contrived death when it violates the human integrity of its victims [capital punishment], but we condemn it when it is an intelligent, voluntary decision."

Before considering the arguments for and against euthanasia, I should make clear that I do not include in this category any imposition of involuntary death by the State. I know there are those who advocate such a practice in dealing with birth monstrosities and people with gross mental defects, but that, it seems to me, does open the door to barbarism.

The foundation of both Catholic and Protestant Christianity's opposition to euthanasia was articulated by Augustine. He argued that any form of suicide is a sin against self, neighbor, and God. "First," he said, "it is contrary to nature: every living organism desires to preserve its life. Second, it is contrary to our social obligation: the whole community is injured. Third, God, alone, should decide when a person will live or die."

To respond to those in inverse order: by that logic, doctors are contravening the "will of God" every time they extend the life of a person by using their medical skill. And what kind of social obligation is rendered when a family's resources are totally exhausted by a lengthy, hopeless hospital stay? The final fact is that it is not contrary to nature for an organism to choose death as preferable to an existence devoid of any pleasure, meaning, or value.

There are more cogent arguments against mercy killing. First, that we never know for certain that an illness is incurable or irreversible. Sometimes, inexplicably, persons get well; I've seen some remarkable recoveries by individuals who, if they'd acted on impulse, might have chosen to end their lives prematurely. More often, however, persons clearly judged by medical experts to be in a process of irreversible deterioration are kept alive for years. Adequate precautions can be taken to protect against a premature judgment of whether recovery is possible.

The other legitimate concern with euthanasia is that widespread, casual practice of it lessens our reverence for life—the same concern as with the casual practice of abortion. The choice is usually not between life and death but whether we grant a humane, dignified death or a slow, humiliating process of deterioration. My personal feeling, which I would not impose on anyone else, is that when my existence becomes incapable of relationship, communication, and conscious thought, I want it to end. We must each draw the line below which the quality of our lives is no longer bearable. The right to life with dignity should be as inalienable as any other.

I suggest two changes in the laws of our states which are needed to support this right of choice for the incurably ill. The first would require hospitals to withhold cardiopulmonary resuscitation and other "heroic measures" from patients who state that this is their desire. It would also give protection to health professionals who obey such an order made in advance by a patient. It would allow a designated surrogate to make that decision after the patient becomes incompetent and hopelessly ill.

I would go further, toward the practice in Holland, with a law which allows the physician, after consulting another doctor, to accelerate the coming of death by merciful means. Again, it would require reasonable certainty that the illness is incurable, and clear evidence that a peaceful death was the patient's wish.

Perhaps the most important achievement of such laws would be that of bringing this matter out of the closet of clandestine decision-making which now happens daily in hospitals, and into the light of honest, caring discussion.

If you have walked through the wards of hospitals where endless suffering continues without purpose; if you have spent time in the urine-soaked halls of nursing homes and gazed into the vacant face of senility, then you must wonder when maintaining life is still humane. Though the heart protests and the mind leaps after simple solutions, there are none. However, our present ambiguity and hypocrisy are not worthy of us. Our failure to confront this issue, caringly, is a national disgrace, and our avoidance of this ethical dilemma is callously cruel.

If we have any genuine reverence for life, we must find a better way of handling hopeless illness and preserving the inalienable right to life—with dignity. "Death is not the enemy. Inhumanity is."

PERSONAL ISSUES

Chronos and Kairos:
It's About Time

A WORD HAS NO TANGIBLE REALITY.
It exists only as a symbol, created to communicate a dimension of human experience. Some words, *percepts,* designate primary, sensory experience. Another kind of word, a *concept,* designates not physical experience but a secondary level of awareness involving intellectual conception. Thus the word *percept* is itself a concept.

Still another kind of word is what's called a *fiction,* which is not a falsehood but an intellectual construct. It refers to a third level of experience and, by naming or describing that experience, it strives to bring order, pattern, and harmony to our lives. The word *truth* is such a symbol for logical order, or rational harmony. *Beauty* is similarly our word for an experience of aesthetic order, or physical harmony. And *goodness* refers to our sense of social order, patterns of behavior which foster social harmony.

Similarly, the word *God* is an intellectual construct, historically used to designate the Source and explain the presence of seemingly purposeful patterns in human existence. Emerson's phrase, "That Reality whose triple face they are . . . ," suggests that truth, beauty, and goodness are dimensions to the character of what we term Deity.

Another intellectual construct—another fiction—is the word *time*. Time itself, like the word, has no objective reality apart from the human mind. It is merely a way of ordering our experience. And though the English language has only one word to represent that endeavor, there are two ways to think about the experience of time. The Greeks had a word for each of them.

The "chronos" sense of time, from which the word *chronology* derives, is simply an effort to structure our experience of physical change with orderly and uniform measurements of the intervals between events. Thus, if there were no physical changes experienced, there would be no experience of chronological time.

Indeed, the intellectual construct we call *time* is based upon the regular repetition of certain observable, physical events— specifically the rotation of the earth, the revolutions of the moon around the earth, and the revolutions of the earth around the sun. All timing devices, from the primitive sundial to sophisticated electronic clocks and calendars, are efforts to convert our experience of the duration between those events into manageable, spatial units. And so we devise the idea of a year to designate the interval between revolutions of the earth around the sun, and a day to signify a full rotation of the earth.

Then we arbitrarily divide that day in twenty-four hours, each hour into sixty minutes, and so forth, clocking our experience to give greater order to our days.

But the whole undertaking depends upon the measurement of objects in space, and our observations are affected by their distance and the speed of light. What our powerful new telescopes "see" happening on a distant star is not what is happening there now. They show us events which occurred years ago and, traveling at 186,000 miles per second, are just now reaching our vision. A closer-to-home example is the fact that we experience thunder following lightning because light travels faster than sound, but the objective reality is that they originate simultaneously.

Science tells us that time and space are relative, that "time stands still" for something traveling at the speed of light, a statement which reflects the artificiality of the intellectual construct and the fact that time has no absolute or objective reality.

More importantly for our daily lives, the "chronos" conception of time, by structuring experience into abstract modules, has substituted something as mechanical as a metronome for the natural, pulsing rhythm of living organisms. There are, of course, material benefits derived from the quantification of time, but at what price have we gained this higher standard of living? We have become slaves to the invention, allowing our lives to be tyrannically governed by what the poet e. e. cummings called "a hoax of clocks and calendars," that dictates when we should eat and sleep and work and play. More important, with the chronos conception of time, we have accepted a linear sense of existence which lives in constant fear of extinction when the sands run down and the clock stops.

So Rudyard Kipling enjoins us to "Fill the unforgiving minute with sixty seconds worth of distance run." Our frantic activism becomes a breathless flight from what's been described as the grim reaper. It is an apt characterization of the spectre of chronos in our lives: like the ancient Greek god, Cronos, who ate his offspring, that sense of time devours every mother's child.

There is another way to think about time. It is reflected in Ecclesiastes. "For everything there is a season and a time to every purpose under heaven: a time to be born . . . and a time to die . . . ," a statement which later concludes, "and everything is beautiful in its time." This "kairos" conception of time, which literally means "the opportune moment," orders life not by the artificial cadence of clocks and calendars but by a qualitative sense of what the moment calls for. It strives to fulfill the occasion rather than fight the fleeting seconds.

Whereas chronos concentrates on the experience of duration, the intervals between events, kairos focuses on the events themselves and a sense of timeliness in our response to them. It defines wisdom as an understanding of the appropriate time, the right moment for rendering meaning and value to life.

In short, kairos is experiential, rather than abstract; it does not march to the beat of an alien pacemaker but moves with the seasonal cycles of nature's rhythms. And it knows that the linear notion of life is an illusion, just as in nature there is no finality, but only an endless process of change in which nothing is ever lost. There is no beginning and end, only a vast cosmic process of transformation in which we may participate. Like the water that evaporates from the earth and returns again as rain, we are part of the cyclical character of nature, ever changing and always renewed in kaleidoscopic patterns of life's energy.

The kairos conception of time reminds us that life cannot be sliced into segments of twenty-four hours and diced into minutes of equal moment. It can only be lived or not lived. And we live it by throwing off the tyranny of chronos and responding fully to the moment at hand.

All of which is illustrated in a parable told by the Buddha. A traveler, fleeing a tiger, ran until he came to a cliff. There he caught hold of a thick vine and swung himself over the edge. Above him the tiger snarled, and below him awaited a long and fatal fall. Two mice appeared, a white one and a black one, and they began to gnaw at the vine. Then, in front of him, the man saw a bunch of grapes. Holding onto the vine with one hand, he picked a grape with the other one and ate it. It tasted delicious.

"To Be Nobody Else But Yourself"

PERSONAL INTEGRITY IS A UNIVER-
sally acclaimed virtue. Socrates prayed for it, asking, "May [my]
inner and outer [character] be one." Shakespeare's Polonius
urged it upon his son: "To thine own self be true. . . . " Emerson
contended that "Nothing at last is sacred but the integrity of
your own mind." The only contrary quotation I could find on
this subject was Mark Twain's suggestion that "To ask some
people to be themselves is the worst advice you can give them!"

My favorite statement on this subject is e. e. cummings's:
"To be nobody else but yourself—in a world which is doing its
best, night and day, to make you everybody else—is to fight the
hardest battle any human being can fight—and never stop
fighting."

Why is integrity so important? Why is it so difficult? How can we overcome the obstacles to integrity and begin the process of becoming nobody else but ourselves?

The answer to the first question is that integrity is important because our health and well-being require it.

It's not merely a matter of failing to fulfill our identity, as was the case with Willy Loman in *Death of a Salesman,* whose son said at his grave, "He never knew who he was." The further fact is that people who are not true to their inner identity become psychologically sick and prone to destructive behavior. One of the "Gnostic Gospels" attributed to Thomas puts it this way: "If you bring forth what is within you, it will save you. If you do not bring forth what is within you, it will destroy you!" The psychologist Rollo May explains the thought with these words: "If any organism fails to fulfill its potentialities, it becomes sick, just as your legs would wither if you never walked."

Integrity is important also because without it we cannot experience meaningful relationships. There is no one there to relate to. And because relationship is one of the greatest sources of joy in life, it is a tragic loss to be incapable of it.

For most of us, however, integrity is not a case of either/or, but more a matter of the degree of integrity we achieve or fail to achieve, and a settling for superficial relationships when our hearts crave something more.

As to the obstacles to achieving integrity, I think there are three major ones. The first is the external reality, alluded to in cummings's statement that the "world is doing its best, night and day, to make you everybody else." Emerson observed this pressure toward conformity when he said, "Society everywhere is in conspiracy against the individuality of its members." We are also conditioned by a religious ethic which says that selflessness is virtuous, and self-sacrifice is the path to salvation.

Using the "I-Thou" conception of Martin Buber, our culture

rightly rejects the practice of I-it relationships in which we use another person as a thing. But in exalting self-sacrifice, the religious ethic fails to recognize that an it-Thou relationship in which we deny our own identity is just as bad.

A reflection of the destructiveness of such behavior is given by Erich Fromm's description of "the unselfish mother." "The children do not show the happiness of persons who are convinced that they are loved; they are anxious, tense, afraid of the mother's disapproval . . . There is nothing more conducive to giving a child the experience of what love, joy, and happiness are than being loved by a mother who loves herself."

Thus, what children need most from their parents is a model of an authentic self-fulfilled and self-loving person. And parents who sacrifice their selves for their children not only abandon their own identities, but also fail to fulfill the children's needs. The same holds true, of course, for every human relationship. Nonetheless, it's difficult in our culture to express such "self-love" because we've been conditioned to feel that virtue lies in self-denial.

The more common obstacle to integrity, however, is an internal, not external, reality: our emotional need to be "well liked," as Willy Loman put it, our fear of rejection and loneliness.

To be nobody but ourselves is to risk such rejection and make ourselves vulnerable to the pain of isolation. It is safer to suppress at least those aspects of our personality which might offend others, to wear a mask that conceals our faults and weaknesses. And, of course, the greater our lack of self-esteem, the less we dare reveal who we are. Achieving integrity requires the risk of self-disclosure.

The third, more profound difficulty in achieving integrity arises from confusion regarding which self we should be faithful to, for we're all comprised of many potential selves, some of which fit Mark Twain's negative description. Hitler, for example, had integrity, but what a perverse self he was consistently expressing.

Peer Gynt, in Ibsen's play, put it this way: "The Gyntian Self!—an army, that—of wishes, appetites, desires—a sea of fancies, claims and aspirations." In the end Peer Gynt realizes that by indiscriminately following the principle of "self-interest" he had failed to recognize the essentials of his real self, and lost the very thing he sought to preserve.

Achieving genuine integrity requires a clear sense of who we truly and totally are, and most of us have not yet developed that awareness.

How do we overcome these formidable obstacles to integrity, and begin the process of becoming nobody else but ourselves? I've already suggested an answer to the cultural conditioning which exacts conformity and exalts self-sacrifice. It is the simple fact that if we do not affirm ourselves, we have nothing to give to anyone else. But obviously this has to be more than an intellectual understanding to be effective. What we have to feel, at a deep, emotional level, is an awareness that our authentic self is the only thing we have to give to another person. It is the one imperishable gift we can make to life itself. We should dread self-betrayal as we would death itself, for that's what it is. In the words of Jean Valjean in *Les Miserables,* "It is a terrible thing to die, but more horrible still is never to have lived."

Regarding the second obstacle to integrity, our fear of rejection and loneliness: it is overcome by a realization that, against the risk which self-disclosure carries, there is a certainty that failure to be ourselves dooms us to the abject aloneness of non-being.

Again, for most of us it's not an either/or decision but a matter of developing a greater degree of integrity. And the wonderful paradox is that our caring relationships, which require some measure of personal identity, also nurture and help us define and develop that identity.

An explorer once came upon a long rope bridge over a deep chasm. He asked a native how the people were able to construct such a bridge, and was told that they began by flying a kite across the abyss to another native. Once the kite string had been caught, a rope was tied to it, then a larger rope until the whole bridge could be pulled into place and secured. So it is with our ventures toward integrity. Small efforts to be faithful to ourselves strengthen our capacity for greater assertions of individuality. We need a little help from our friends, as the song says, but it all begins with our determined decision to be nobody else but ourselves.

The final obstacle to that endeavor is more difficult to overcome. And it often takes a lifetime. Among the many, sometimes conflicting, "fancies, claims and aspirations," how do we discover our true selves?

To some extent, it's simply a matter of trial and error: assuming an identity and seeing how it fits. That practice requires a willingness to recognize when we have made an error, deal with the consequences, and change our understanding of who we are.

Discovering ourselves also involves a shedding of socially-imposed role-identities which we had internalized. That is what the women's liberation movement is about, and it has great significance for men, also. If we want the freedom to be ourselves, we must abandon the masculine and feminine stereotypes which would circumscribe the dimensions of our identities.

The crucial recognition is that our true selves are, whatever else, interconnected, interdependent entities. Milton Sapirstein put it this way: " 'To thine own self be true' is a wise admonition when the self is understood to be what in fact it is, an unbelievably complex focus of needs and drives which must be brought into balance, not only with each other but with the world outside the self. We are, as it were, in the center of an immense web, a series of interlocking relationships which range from ego, through the intimate members of our family circle, our friends, to society at large, and finally to humanity itself."

In short, there is no "self" to be expressed and no self-fulfillment to be found apart from a context of loyalties and commitments. Recognizing that fact is the first step toward true integrity and being "nobody else but yourself."

Trust Your Tears

I N A MUSEUM IN JERUSALEM THERE IS A display case which contains a collection of tiny cups. When asked their purpose, the guide explained that the little ceramic goblets were sacramental vessels. They were not employed in public religious ceremonies, but were for personal use. People cried into them. At times of great sorrow or great joy, when tears came forth, they were caught and kept on the mantel of a home. What the original owners of the cups were saying is that tears are precious, they show that you care. They remind us of the times we cared so deeply about something that we wept.

In a society where caring enough means to send the very best Hallmark cards, it would be well for us to learn from those ancient Jews to treasure our tears.

There is a tendency in our culture to distrust tears: to trivialize and suppress them. Think about the last time you cried. How did you feel about it? Most people are embarrassed and seek to stifle the flow as quickly as possible. Every minister has counseled persons whose troubles warrant sorrow and crying. But when the tears come, they apologize for "breaking down," sigh deeply to suppress the tears and strive mightily to compose themselves.

Why do we do this? We all do. Men have a particularly hard time expressing their sorrows or their moments of great joy with weeping. That's why they are more prone to heart attacks. We resist crying because we are afraid of our feelings. We don't want to lose control. We don't want to appear weak. We don't want to risk the vulnerability of caring that much. Our fantasy is that if we let go and allow the tears to flow, we will never stop crying, or that we will do something foolish.

The reality is that nothing is more foolish and self-destructive than suppressed feeling. Our concern with appearing weak ignores the fact that those who stifle their feelings are truly weakened. The suppression of emotion leaves us bereft of the source of our power. It is a sign of strength to be sensitive and caring and capable of expressing emotion. And vulnerability, which literally means "susceptible to being wounded," is an index of aliveness. Only those who never love never risk the loss of a loved one. Only those who never feel avoid the pain of suffering. Only those who have never lived avoid the sorrow of dying.

Consider the story of Father Damien, the Catholic priest who went to Molokai to live with the lepers. For thirteen years he worked with them as a friend and spiritual counselor, and then finally contracted leprosy and died. This is the circumstance under which he discovered that he had the disease: one morning he spilled boiling water on his foot and didn't feel it. His lack of sensation told him he was doomed.

86

If you have not recently felt tears of sorrow in this anguished world, do not congratulate yourself. The absence of pain is no proof of the presence of health. It may be the evidence of a loss of sensitivity which is a form of death.

We must learn to treasure and trust our tears for they have much to teach us.

First, they teach us that life is essentially tragic—not merely often unfair, but intrinsically tragic. We don't want to believe this. We rebel against it and sometimes our noblest acts spring from such rebellion. But as someone once wrote, "For those who think, life is comic. For those who feel, life is tragic."

A little girl, standing on a curb and looking at a mud-puddle in which an oil slick was making iridescent colors, said, "Oh, look, Mother, there's a rainbow gone to smash." Life is like that. It's a weird mixture of happiness and heartache, of triumphs and failures, of high hopes and rainbows gone to smash. Somewhere on our way to mature adulthood, we recognize that all our triumphs are transitory, all our satisfactions are temporary, all our relationships are imperfect and subject to sudden termination. It is a "given," built into the nature of human consciousness, that our intellectual reach exceeds our grasp, that we yearn for that which can never be fully realized, that death is the ultimate manifestation of the fact that there are no permanent victories.

Walt Whitman wrote of animals: "They do not lie awake in the dark and weep . . . " Of course not. Animals live without the blessing and curse of human consciousness. The high hazard of being human, the deepest spring from which our tears flow, is an awareness of the vast gulf between what we can imagine and what life is. When we tearfully recognize that this existential condition is something we share with every other human being, a bond of kinship can be established that makes life not only bearable but sometimes even joyous.

Our tears can also teach us what really matters. They are often the saline solution which clears our vision of life's enduring values. Indeed, we cry when we are confronted with either the loss of, or the beautiful moving expression of, that which we most value; so crying is always revealing of what matters. If you want to know what you truly prize, keep a diary of your deepest disappointments and highest joys. To paraphrase Jesus, "where your treasure is, there will be your tears also." What are the values that most often evoke the tears of joy and sorrow? An African pygmy chief named Kitabu once eloquently expressed them: "If you give a piece of your heart to things that you own, you cannot love people with all of your heart. You become the slave of the things that you own. We love and take care of people, not things. The whites think we are poor. Let them think what they please! Happiness is the smile on the face of your wife when you bring home the antelope. Happiness is the laughter of your children. Happiness is the music you make. Happiness is freedom. These are not things that you own—they are things you enjoy."

Another reflection of what really matters in life was written by Roland de Pury, the minister of a small church in Lyons, France, during the Nazi occupation of that country. One summer Sunday morning in 1942 he was seized and taken to prison for eight months. Shut in a cell by himself, the door locked and even the small window covered, he later wrote: "I was alone. My only way out was a door I could not open. I would gladly have chosen to be beaten, starved, or tortured—if it would but permit me fifteen minutes conversation with a human being." Eight months after that fateful Sunday, the door opened. His name was called. He was to be freed on a prisoner exchange. He describes his first meal in the world of the living: "The words of Thanksgiving before that meal were no mere formality but the stammering of men drunk with pure gratitude . . . I went up to my room. My room, not my cell. Then I opened and shut the door—and opened and shut the door—and opened and shut the door again. I was rich! I staggered with the wealth of a door that would open under my own hand."

Our tears can teach us what matters in life.

Finally, our tears can drive us to discover the deeper sources of comfort available to every human being. The word "comfort," from the Latin "cum forte," literally means "with strength." And there is, deep inside every one of us, a strength greater than we ever dreamed, a strength which is discovered only when we are driven to the extremities of feeling. Such strength comes not in response to a solicitous soothing that would shelter us from life's tragic dimensions. It is most evoked, from the recesses of our own being, when we are challenged to break out of the prison of our self-centered sorrow and demonstrate to the world that "death shall have no dominion" over our souls, nor shall any tragedy break our spirits.

My colleague, Robert Weston, once put it well:

Shall I tell you where there is comfort?
Not in the warm bed,
Nor at the table with food piled high;
Not in the promise that our tears shall be wiped away
And our wounds healed,
But that we weep for that which is worth weeping:
That our wounds were gained in warfare for a cause
Which shall live in the hearts of people when we
    are gone.

The ancient Jews were wise to treasure their tears. They teach us that life is essentially tragic, that what matters most is a loving relationship, that there is strength to be found in a sensitized awareness. Trust your tears.

The Subtle
Sin of Envy

SHAKESPEARE CALLED IT "THE GREEN sickness," thereby coloring our language for the trait ever since. The writer Horace said, "Sicilian tyrants never invented a greater torment than that of envy." And the New Testament Letter of James suggested that it is "The source of all our feuding and quarreling." The phenomenon is as old as Adam and Eve and as contemporary as you and me.

Why do we envy? Dante described the envious in Purgatory as blind: "their eyes were sewn shut." It isn't clear whether they are blind because of their envy, or envious because they are blind. I contend that both conditions are true.

People whose gaze is forever fixed on what other people possess are incapable of seeing the potential sources of value all around them. And it is when we cannot recognize the sources of joy available to us that we are inclined to envy what others have.

This results partially from distorted values. What do we usually envy? Someone else's wealth, or looks, or fame. All of these may be enjoyable, but are they really so necessary to a happy life?

Years ago in *The Hidden Persuaders,* Vance Packard commented on American advertising practices with these examples: a happy family standing before a long, long car proclaimed proudly, "We're not wealthy. We just look it!" But the best illustration of the silliness of such value confusion is the caption on a two-page full-color ad picturing a family driving up to an expensive home: "They'll know you've arrived when you drive up in an Edsel."

If you're inclined to envy the rich, here is a bit of historical lore: In 1923, the world's most successful financiers met in Chicago. Together they controlled more wealth than the U.S. Treasury. What happened to them? "The Wall Street Bear," Jesse Livermore, committed suicide. The president of the International Bank, Leon Fraser, committed suicide. The head of the world's largest monopoly, Ivar Krueger, committed suicide. Steel company president Charles Schwab lived the last five years of his life in poverty. The wheat speculator, Arthur Cutton, also died penniless. And the head of the New York Stock Exchange spent the last years of his life in jail.

Reflecting another focus of misplaced emphasis, a sorority applicant was asked to describe her most outstanding asset. She simply listed the numbers: "38-26-36." Our emphasis on physical beauty is, clearly, a matter of value confusion. The best illustration was the popular envy of Marilyn Monroe, whose life was so lonely, empty, and unhappy that she finally committed suicide.

When we magnify superficial values, we become blind to the more enduringly significant sources of joy available to every one of us.

We also are inclined toward envy when self-doubt and lack of self-esteem blind us to our capacity for generating the values which are important: integrity of character, friendship, and creative accomplishment. There is, of course, room for a healthy humility. Joe Louis, the boxing champion, once visited a boys' trade school and admired the things the young men had made, saying, "I always wished I could do something with my hands." The ability to distinguish between creative and destructive talent is a value clarity borne of honest self-awareness.

Sir Walter Scott exhibited the same capacity. He had been widely regarded as the greatest poet of his generation, and then Byron came on the scene with a brilliance that cast Scott in the shadows. An anonymous reviewer praised Byron extravagantly and described him as a better poet than Scott. Some time later it was revealed that the review was written by Scott himself. The more secure you are in your own self-worth the more able you are to admire others without envy. We tend to envy when we are blind to our own capacity for generating things of value.

What happens when we envy? Why do I call it a sin? At the most obvious level envy is sinful because it dissipates our energies in longing. Blinded by our discontent, we do not use whatever talent we have creatively, but spend it on the effort to appropriate what someone else has. The classic illustration of this behavior is Shakespeare's Iago. He so covets Othello's fame that he is driven to employ his considerable genius to destroy his rival.

At a deeper, more significant level, envy distorts our identity, and because we then fail to fulfill our potential selves, it is sinfully wrong. In the Book of Job it is written: "Wrath kills a foolish man. Envy slays a silly one." That's true. How silly, as well as sad, to be so consumed with envy that we destroy our own unique identities. "There comes a time in everyone's education," Emerson wrote, "when we recognize that envy is ignorance, that imitation is suicide."

I want to distinguish here, again, between admiration, which can be healthy, and envy which is not. Alexander Pope put it well: "Envy—to which the ignoble mind is slave—is emulation to the learned or brave." It is indeed wise and brave to emulate good and great human beings: doing so develops our own worth. The difference is that admiration preserves our integrity. Envy is a sin because it dissipates our energies and destroys our identity.

Now, to the more difficult task of prescribing for "the green sickness." (The phrase is apt because it suggests a life which, like unripened fruit, is unfulfilled.) How do we deal with our inclination toward envy? To the degree that a distortion of values is involved, we must strive to regain our perspective on what's really important, to undertake a values clarification exercise.

A blind woman had much to teach us regarding the things of worth we fail to see. Helen Keller once wrote a magazine piece entitled "Three Days to See" in which she said: "If I were granted sight for three days ... the first day would be a busy one. I should call to me all my dear friends and look into their faces, imprinting on my mind the outward evidence of the beauty within them. ... I should also view the small, simple things of my home. I want to see the warm colors of the rugs under my feet, the pictures on the walls, the intimate trifles that transform a house into a home. I should take a long walk in the woods and fill my eyes with the beauties of the world of nature ... and pray for the glory of a colorful sunset. When dusk had fallen I should experience the double delight of being able to see by artificial light. ... In the night of that first day of sight, I should not be able to sleep—so full would be my mind of the sweet memories of the day."

If hearing that statement prompts you to envy the perceptiveness of Helen Keller, recognize that you can cultivate such awareness for yourself. It'll take some effort. Contrary to the song, the best things in life are not free. Indeed it is when we recognize that everything worth having in life is available to us if we are willing to pay the price, that we are grown-up emotionally. Instead of waiting around for someone to bring us flowers, we must plant our own garden.

The other antidote to "the green sickness" is, of course, that of strengthening self-awareness. Satchel Paige put it plainly: "Not everyone is born great, but there ain't no one gotta be common."

How true. No one is so lacking in significance that he or she is better off being a carbon copy of someone else. Every human being has a unique worth that can be expressed. The task of life is to find out what that is. During World War II, when sugar was rationed, a restaurant customer who had already been given his share called for more sugar for his coffee. The waitress's answer was a classic for brevity and wisdom, "Stir what you've got."

As Jesus put it, "The Kingdom of Heaven is within you." We don't need to envy others; everything we need to have a happy, full, and meaningful life exists in us right now, waiting to be expressed.

Aldous Huxley elaborated on the thought in these words: "It is because we don't know who we are, because we are unaware that the Kingdom of Heaven is within us, that we behave in the generally silly, the often insane, the sometimes criminal ways that are so characteristically human. We are saved, we are liberated and enlightened by perceiving the hitherto unperceived good that is already within us."

Cultivating the
Value of Loneliness

W_{E ALL NEED TO LOVE AND TO BE}
loved. But equally important is the significance of loneliness.
The paradoxical fact is that loneliness and relatedness are not
opposites but complementary facets of a whole and satisfying
life.

I point this out because many people seem to be driven by
loneliness anxiety—a dread of being alone so great that it drives
them toward all kinds of foolish behavior, which leaves them
more estranged. Some escape into alcohol, some into superficial
sexual adventures; others rush into ill-considered marriages;
still others engage in a compulsive busyness on the assumption
that, if they cram every waking moment with activity, they

won't be lonely. Like native drums beaten to ward off evil spirits, the incessant chatter of superficial activities is maintained to drive off the haunting specter of loneliness. We surround ourselves with the sounds of life to keep from experiencing the solitariness of silence.

But I contend that to explore our loneliness rather than run away from it is to discover our true selves, to experience the basis of meaningful relationships, and to discover the deeper dimensions of life. It is only in solitary, lonely reflection that we discover our selves, that we find the unique identity without which we cannot love or be loved. Andre Gide, the French author, said it best: "Many people suffer so from the fear of finding themselves alone that they never find themselves at all!"

We human beings do employ a variety of clever devices for running away from ourselves. Our modern world is abundant with such escapist stratagems, and by the middle of life most of us are accomplished fugitives. The irony is that the reason we can't bear to be alone is that we derive our sense of identity from encounter with others. We depend upon interpersonal contact to define our self-awareness, using people like a mirror to reflect the image of who we are.

This is understandable and may even be necessary in our immature years. The truth we must eventually learn is that no one else can give us our identity. It has to emerge from within. If we have no sense of selfhood apart from our contact with others, we will be incapable of meaningful relationships. There will be no one there to relate to.

It is often said that a camel is a horse that was put together by a committee. Well, if we allow a committee of our family and friends to define our identity, it will be like a camel. Although it is true that an encounter with another person will sometimes stimulate self-discovery, such self-awareness is always the later product of solitary reflection. We can fashion the unique identity which is ours only when we explore the recesses of our own being. And that's something we have to do alone.

To evade the experience of loneliness also results in an estrangement from other human beings. For to suppress such awareness is to deny the fundamental, common condition of our humanity. A "Peanuts" cartoon depicts one of the children asking, "What are you going to be when you grow up, Charlie Brown?" With infinite pathos in his look, Charlie replies, "Lonely." Thomas Wolfe stated the matter more fully: "Loneliness, far from being a rare and curious phenomenon, is the central and inevitable fact of human existence." That's true; no human being is ever completely known or understood by another. And our efforts at forming attachments are conditioned by that fact.

If you are feeling sorry for yourself because that is true, that no one else really understands what you are feeling, remember that it is true of everyone. The glorious thing about a genuinely loving relationship is that, though it cannot destroy that gulf between persons, it can transcend the chasm at least momentarily. It can express a capacity for caring acceptance of that which can never be fully known or understood. But unless you have explored your own loneliness, you will not be able to experience such love.

The common tragedy is that so many of us, in our aversion to pain and suppression of suffering, have rendered ourselves incapable of empathizing with someone else's experience of sorrow or grief. Our relationships remain shallow and superficial: there is no depth of common feeling because we have avoided our common experience. An old Hassidic tale asks, "How can you love me if you do not know what causes me pain?" I would add, "How can you know what gives me pain if you have not experienced it?"

To recognize the fact of our loneliness, and experience the pain of it, is to discover kindredness with all other human beings—a foundation for the joy of the relationship. So let there be loneliness, for where there is loneliness there is sensitivity, and where there is sensitivity, there is awareness and recognition and promise.

Finally, it is in our solitariness that we discover the deeper, enduring values of life—the truth and beauty and meaning which is glimpsed only by those who cultivate the inner spaces of their being. Nietzsche put it this way: "If you can read your own life, you can understand the hieroglyphics of universal life." What is true for you, in the deepest part of your being, is true for all persons. But it is only in solitary searching that such understanding is experienced.

Similarly, regarding creativity, John Steinbeck wrote: "Our species is the only creative species, and it has only one creative instrument: the individual mind and spirit. Nothing was ever created by two persons. There are no good collaborations— whether in music, in art, in poetry, mathematics, or philosophy. Once the miracle of creation has taken place, the group can build and extend it, but the group never invents anything. That preciousness lies in the lonely mind . . . of [a human being]."

That is why beauty has more to do with integrity than with prettiness. Only the artist who is faithful to the inward vision, discovered in solitude, can express truth and beauty which are universally recognized as authentic.

When I speak of these things as entities experienced in the depths of lonely reflection, I am discussing dimensions of a Reality which has historically been termed God. I have no need to personify the Reality, but I believe that it exists and is the source of life's meaning. It is an ineffable but very real "Ground of Being" which is essential to life with pattern and purpose. A Quaker, Thomas Kelly, said it well: "Deep within us all there is an amazing inner sanctuary, a Holy Place, a divine center, to which we may continuously return. Eternity is at our hearts, pressing upon our time-worn lives, warming us with intimations of an astounding destiny, calling us home—unto itself. Yielding to these persuasions, gladly committing ourselves in body and soul, utterly and completely to the light within . . . is the beginning of true life." Such awareness is known only by those who have cultivated the value of loneliness.

An ancient legend tells of a man walking late one night who suddenly came upon a large black cat. He was seized with fear and turned to walk away from this ominous creature. It followed him, and he began to run. When he looked back, it seemed to grow larger and more menacing until it became a huge, ferocious panther. He became exhausted and could run no further. He decided he would have to turn, face the monster, and deal with it as best he could. But when he did, the cat stopped also. And when he took a step toward it, the cat began to retreat, growing smaller and smaller as he followed it, until the fearful beast became a playful, purring kitten which curled in his lap and nuzzled against his hands. So it is with the experience of loneliness.

Is Love the
Every Only God?

EVERY YEAR OUR NATION CELEBRATES
Valentine's Day and gives deference, if not worship, to Eros, the
ancient god of Greek mythology. All across the land bells ring—
on the cash registers of candy stores and flower shops—in
honor of the deity of romantic love.

Most people would insist that in celebrating the significance
of love, they are not committing the blasphemy of equating its
power with that of God. But our behavior makes it a serious
question. We sigh for love, we cry for love, we lie for love, and
sometimes even die for love—reflecting its enormous power
over our lives.

I want to establish a common definition of love, since the
term has been so misused, as people proclaim their love for

everything from strawberries to God. Rollo May provides us with a comprehensive description of the reality in a book entitled *Love and Will*: "There are four kinds of love in Western tradition: sex, or libido; eros, the drive to create; philia, or friendship; and agape, unconditional devotion to the welfare of the other." Every human experience of authentic love, Dr. May insists, "is a blending in varying proportions of these four."

I would emphasize that fact in my use of the term. Genuine love always includes: physical affection, commitment to creativity, friendly concern, and radical acceptance. You cannot say you love someone you don't even like, and use the word accurately. Nor can a relationship which is not concerned with the growth of the other person be appropriately described as love. By the same token, authentic love is under a compulsion to express itself physically—if only by a warm handshake. What happens when it isn't expressed is illustrated in the story of a young man who was separated from his sweetheart for a year. He wrote her every day and, at the end of that time, she married the letter carrier.

I want to focus on "Eros," the creative dimension of love. I quote again from Dr. May, who distinguishes between Eros and sex: "Eros created life on the earth, the early Greek mythology tells us. When the world was barren and lifeless, it was Eros who seized his life-giving arrows, pierced the cold bosom of the Earth, and immediately the brown surface was covered with luxuriant verdure. This is an appealing symbolic picture of how Eros incorporates sex—those phallic arrows which pierce—as the instrument by which he creates life." "Eros," says Joseph Campbell, "is always, regardless of guise, the progenitor, the original creator from which life comes."

It is the latter contention that I would explore. If Eros is the creator from which life comes, is it true, as e. e. cummings suggests, that "love is the every only God / which spoke this

104

world so glad and big"? Is the concept of "God" simply "a poetic projection," a symbol for the creative power of love which is the true source and sustenance of life?

The contention is not totally foreign to Judeo-Christian theology. In the New Testament Letter of John, the writer contends that "God is love and whoever abides in love abides in God." But of course that was meant to describe a dimension of the deity, not its totality. He didn't say "love is God," but that in love relationship we experience the crucial characteristic of the creator.

Recently, belief in a supernatural being has become, for many, less and less tenable. It is difficult to reconcile the traditional conception of deity as all-powerful and loving with the fact of evil in the world. As "J.B." put it in MacLeish's play, "If God is good [loving], he is not God [all powerful]."

Many people, including writers like D. H. Lawrence, have concluded that there is no "God" out there. They contend that the Reality we objectify with that word resides in us and our capacity for caring. Alfred North Whitehead, the founder of "process theology," put it this way: "God is in the world or nowhere, creating continually in us and around us. This creative principle is a continuing process, and insofar as we partake of [it] we partake of the divine ... [and experience] our true destiny as co-creators of the universe."

In this context, the problem of evil is seen as a reflection of the fact that we live in an evolving, unfinished universe which awaits the efforts of our hands and hearts. Well, how do we feel about that possibility? Is love the one true "God"? There is much merit to the idea—and a grave danger.

It is certainly true that love performs many functions historically ascribed to deity. We are literally created by sexual love, nurtured toward growth by the challenge of Eros, comforted by friendly companionship, and freed to be our unique selves by someone's unconditional acceptance. Love, someone wrote, is the capacity to respond to the potentialities of another person. Experiencing such responsiveness releases us from self-doubt and frees us for the expression of our unique identities. It also enlarges our capacity for caring about others. Because we have been loved, we can love others and be responsive to their needs.

Love also fosters what traditional theologians have called "atonement," a word which Erich Fromm transliterates "at-one-ment," an overcoming of our sense of separation from "the ground of being."

The Jewish theologian Martin Buber explains the thought: "Divine reality exists between persons. The true meaning of love one's neighbor is not that it is a commandment from God, which we are to fulfill, but that through it and in it we meet God." "We become whole," he explains later, "only by virtue of relation to another self." It is this concept of wholeness which is more meaningful to many. They see love as "the every only God" because it is continually reconnecting all creatures big and small in one holy creation.

Thus, it is the creative power of human relationship, not some theological abstraction, that overcomes the tragic aspects of existence and makes life worth living. That is why "Hell," as Dostoevski wrote, "is the suffering of being unable to love."

Finally, love functions, as God has traditionally been thought to function, by bringing the element of judgment to our lives. As Kahlil Gibran poetically describes in *The Prophet,* "Even as [love] is for your growth, so is he for your pruning. Even as he ascends to your height and caresses your tenderest branches that quiver in the sun, so shall he descend to your roots and shake them in their clinging to the earth. All these things shall love do unto you that you may know the secrets of your heart, and in that knowledge become a fragment of Life's heart."

That's true because any truly intimate relationship forces us to confront ourselves more honestly. It's not that the other person is judging us, but that we, confronted by an unconditional love, judge our own unworthiness. Experiencing love, like the ancient mystics' experience of God, is comparable to entering a refining fire. One theologian wrote, "If you've never tried to escape from God, you've never truly experienced God."

Well, whether or not that's true of a supernatural reality, it describes accurately the fact that, though we want love, we tend to run away from its judgment and the risk of self-disclosure it requires. A good case is to be made for the idea that "Love is the every only God" which judges—as well as creates and sustains our lives.

There is also a grave danger in such thinking. "When [people] cannot see God, they make idols," an old truism says, "They worship their own desires." Idolatry means ascribing ultimate and eternal reality to something which is finite—fleeting, something therefore incapable of bearing the burden of such devotion. The god is too small.

How can we test the validity of love as an object of devotion? We can submit it to Rollo May's four-fold definition. If, for example, it does not produce "an urge toward higher forms of being," then it's neither true love nor a worthy representation of the creative power of life. Any exaltation of love must always be tempered by a devotion to truth and justice. Historically, a myopic love of country, which disregards the demands of truth and justice, has demonstrated the destructiveness of such idolatry. The same can be said of a selfish and amoral romantic love. If it makes you feel less caring toward others, it's not worthy of the word.

The creative force we experience in love, with all its power to give us life, may be an appropriate symbol for deity, but no particular relationship deserves that designation, nor should we cling to it as something ultimate and eternal.

POLITICAL CONCERNS

POETICAL CONCERNS

Political Labels

THERE ARE MANY WAYS OF LYING.
Some are blatantly bad, others are more subtle and therefore
worse.

An example of the more sly and sinister prevarication was
written by George Orwell, long before the Vietnam war:
"Defenseless villages are bombarded from the air, the inhabi-
tants driven out into the countryside, their cattle machine-
gunned, their huts set on fire with incendiary bullets, and this is
called pacification." When a pleasant word is used to describe a
not-so-nice reality, it's called a *euphemism,* which is simply a
nice word for lying.

A different method of mendacity (another euphemism for
lying) is that of labeling people and their ideas. There is an old
saying that "We speak of the sins for which we have no mind

111

and avoid the ones toward which we are inclined." The fact is that we are all guilty of this sin. Indeed, I may have to conclude the way Mort Sahl closes his monologues, asking, "Is there anyone here I haven't offended?"

My thesis may be stated in two sentences: Every label tends to be a lie—at best an imprecise tool of language, at worse an insidiously irresponsible weapon of attack. But since they seem to be unavoidable and, perhaps, a necessary form of communication, we ought to define our labels as clearly as we can before we use them.

The need for labels, as linguistic shorthand, stems from our inability to cope with the complexity of questions and deal with them more precisely. A cartoon depicted two cows grazing in a field as a modern milk truck rolled by. The sign on the truck boasted, "Our milk is pasteurized, homogenized, standardized and enriched with vitamin D." One of the cows is saying, "It makes you feel kind of inadequate, doesn't it?"

That's how most of us feel about the complicated issues of modern life, so we generate labels to make them more manageable, neatly pigeon-holing people and ideas. But the first test of the effectiveness of a word as a tool of communication is whether it means the same thing to the listener that it does to the speaker. Labels seldom do.

The term *liberal* could be describing an attitude toward change: open-minded and flexible as opposed to dogmatic and rigid. Or it could be referring to a particular position on an issue: a liberal view held with doctrinaire rigidity—which, of course, is the exact opposite of the first definition.

In the political realm, if we are inclined to use a label in the doctrinaire sense, we must remember that whether a person or a certain view is regarded as liberal or conservative is usually a relative judgment, reflecting the times and the comparable position of the person using the label. What was considered liberal, and often radical, when first proposed by Norman Thomas in the 1920s is now contained in both major party platforms. To maintain those views today is a "conservative" position.

By the same token, we tend to judge someone as liberal or conservative in relation to where we stand on issues. The John Birch Society saw President Eisenhower as pretty far to the left, while many left-wing radicals saw President Kennedy as too conservative. If we return to the first definition of *liberal* as flexible toward change, most of us would have to admit that we are liberal on some issues and conservative on others. An illustration of that fact is the stance which most liberals take on the question of public aid to parochial schools: they don't want to change the historic provision for separation of church and state.

Labels are, at best, imprecise and inaccurate. They purchase simplicity at the price of accuracy. When they are used as a weapon to discredit a person or idea, labels are insidiously irresponsible. They exploit base emotions and encourage mindless behavior which buries reason along with its victim. An apt example is "McCarthyism," admittedly a label coined to describe the Wisconsin senator's practice of destroying people's credibility by fastening the tab *Communist* upon them. It is a tactic as deadly as it is devious because, once tagged, the victim is powerless to vindicate himself; every protest of innocence is suspected of greater duplicity. One of the variations of this "red-baiting" tactic which Senator McCarthy practiced is that of "guilt by association." If someone takes the same position on an issue that a Communist takes, he or she must be "one of them." The same irresponsible tactic is employed when the radical left suggest that, because Hitler was anti-Communist, every anti-Communist is a fascist.

A story which illustrates the irresponsibility of the guilt by association approach tells of a man who had been the village drunk and had reformed. For weeks he had gone without a drink. But one Saturday morning at the town store, the crowd started chiding him about falling off the wagon. He said it was a lie, but they insisted that the word was out. He asked from whom. They pointed to the village gossip as their source. Angrily he went to the woman and accused her of spreading lies. She insisted they were not lies; she had evidence that proved he had started drinking again. What was the evidence? His wheelbarrow had stood in front of the saloon all Friday night. The man answered in actions rather than in words. He parked his wheelbarrow in front of the gossip's house, and left it there all Saturday night. So much for the tactic of guilt by association.

As to political labels, I suggest that we rid ourselves of the right-to-left conception of those positions. I would abandon the notion that to the left of center (wherever that is) we have liberals, then socialists, then communists, and that to the right we have conservatives, then reactionaries, then fascists. Among the many things wrong with such a spectrum is the suggestion that the extremes are opposite. In fact, they are more alike than different. Neither extreme would grant freedom of expression to those who don't share their views; both tend toward conspiracy theories and would use any means to achieve their ends, including lies and violence.

The right-to-left approach also implies that a step toward liberalism is movement toward Communism, and a step toward conservatism is movement toward fascism. Neither is true; the nations in the world which are the most prone to the appeals of Communism are not those with a liberal or socialist history (like Sweden) but those accustomed to authoritarian rule. Similarly, a genuine conservative, who places a high value on individual liberty, is hardly a good candidate for fascist ideals.

114

The first step in clarifying political labels is to rid ourselves of the erroneously misleading right-to-left analogy.

Having done that, how may we meaningfully define liberal and conservative politically? In his *Devil's Dictionary*, Ambrose Bierce suggests that "A conservative is one who is enamored of existing evils, as distinguished from a liberal—who wishes to replace them with others." When I observe the political scene, I sometimes think that distinction may be as good as any.

Let us reject the popular and erroneous characterizations of those positions. They suggest that conservatives are on the side of property rights as opposed to human rights, and liberals are in favor of big government at the expense of individual freedom. Both of those are distortions, examples of irresponsible labeling. Putting property rights above human rights is not genuine conservatism; it's greed. And no intelligent liberal wants unnecessarily to expand the federal bureaucracy; only the power-hungry of both political parties seek that. (Incidentally, it is ironic that those who complain most loudly about big government and taxes also want to increase the military budget and bureaucracy.) It should be obvious to any thoughtful observer that the unbridled exercise of property rights will eventually destroy individual freedoms. The role of government must be that of protecting citizens from exploitation by the powerful greedy.

Some may call it socialism, but the fact is that we cannot return to the limited federal government of the eighteenth century and deal effectively with the complexities of modern society. The government which governs best is not that which governs least, but that which governs most effectively. Responsible liberals and conservatives will both recognize that.

I would suggest a different way of distinguishing between liberal and conservative positions; it's not orthodox, but it's more interesting because it's original. It is based on a belief that every vital issue involves tension between a valid concern for persons and an equally legitimate regard for principles. I would describe a responsible liberal as someone who consistently stresses a regard for the welfare of persons and a responsible conservative as someone who habitually emphasizes the pre-serving of principles. Neither of them disregards the other consideration, but each stresses what seems most important.

A liberal would argue that principles exist only to serve persons. And if in a given situation they do not serve a cause or a human need, they should be altered or abandoned. A conserva-tive would insist that the long-range interests of persons are best served by maintaining time-tested principles, and therefore would tend to resist altering them.

Both are valid emphases and reflect perspectives which any thoughtful person might hold on a given issue. But proponents of unregulated commerce, which allows business to amass huge profits at consumer expense, are not true conservatives. Lobby-ing for the military-industrial complex does not represent true liberalism. Each serves vested interests which seek to profit from such enterprises—with regard for neither persons nor principles.

Thus defining the labels *liberal* and *conservative*, I suggest that there is room for, indeed need for, both kinds of persons in our political life.

Is there anyone out there I haven't offended?

Toward an
Ethic of the Erotic

EVERY SO OFTEN, AN ISSUE ARISES THAT forces us to undertake a values clarification exercise to decide which of several conflicting values is most important to us. Pornography is such an issue, as are abortion, capital punishment, and others which are difficult to deal with rationally until we have identified and ranked the values at stake.

What is pornographic or obscene? And, perhaps more importantly, who decides that it is?

There was a time in our society when any display of the human body was regarded as obscene, when women wore long skirts and sleeves lest their limbs be seen, when the word *legs* was too graphic and provocative for polite conversation. In

117

those days any books which described the sexual act were considered pornographic. In the 1930s, James Joyce's *Ulysses* and D.H. Lawrence's *Lady Chatterley's Lover,* both now considered fine literature, were banned in this country. In 1925 a customs inspector refused to admit two books of photographs. One he listed as entitled, *Ceiling, Sistine* by a Michael Angelo. And not much later, H.L. Mencken was arrested on an obscenity charge because *The American Mercury* magazine, which he edited, carried a short story about a prostitute.

All this began to change in recent years, and in 1957 the Supreme Court, called upon to define the term, made a distinction between "acceptable descriptions of sexuality" and "obscenity" by designating as obscene "material in which the dominant theme, taken as a whole, appeals to prurient interests."

Prurient, according to the dictionary, means "causing lasciviousness." In other words, if it turns you on, it's obscene. The problem with that definition, besides the fact that it implies that sexual desire is bad, is, of course, its subjectivity.

There's an old story that illustrates the inadequacy of such subjective judgment. It tells of a New Yorker who took a visiting friend to the top of the Empire State building and asked him what he thought of the view. "It reminds me of sex," the visitor replied. "How can that skyline remind you of sex?" his host questioned. And the visitor responded, "Oh, that's easy. Everything reminds me of sex!" So it is with some people. How do we define prurient interests for them?

Another illustration of the problem: "The Song of Solomon" in the Bible contains ecstatic descriptions of a woman's breasts and thighs, which must be considered by some as erotic. Should the Bible, therefore, be banned?

In 1966 the Warren Court sought to handle that problem by adding the criterion that the material must be "utterly without redeeming social value." It might turn you on, but if it also has a socially significant message, it's all right—which, presumably, gets the Bible off the hook.

But in 1973 the more conservative Burger Court sought to reverse this reckless tide by ruling that local juries could decide what "offended community standards" and convict—"if the material, taken as a whole, lacked serious literary, artistic, or scientific value."

The problem with that definition is that "community standards" are continually changing and vary so much from place to place. How would community standards be established for movies on transcontinental airplane flights?

Because of that ruling, however, a Georgia court subsequently designated the widely-acclaimed film *Carnal Knowledge* as pornographic and banned its showing. More outrageously, in Memphis, Tennessee, a jury extradited an actor, Harry Reems, had him brought there in handcuffs, and convicted him of conspiracy to commit obscenity because he had appeared in the film *Deep Throat*—even though he had never before been in Memphis.

It is again a subjective judgment which allows jurors to impose their personal values regarding what is offensive to community standards and lacking in artistic or literary merit. Just how subjective that can be is reflected in the famous statement of Justice Potter Stewart who, when asked what hard-core pornography was, said, "I may not be able to define it, but I know it when I see it!"

There is clearly no objective definition of obscenity or pornography upon which to base a judgment regarding censorship. How then do we decide if and when sexually explicit material should be banned? It seems to me that the only valid basis for such a serious infringement on civil liberties is whether or not the material is harmful to human beings. First

119

amendment freedoms of speech and expression are not absolute. You cannot, for example, shout fire in a crowded theater, or libel someone with impunity. But the legitimacy of such restrictions must always rest on a clear and present danger of harm to human beings.

What is the public harmfulness of sexually explicit material? This was one of the specific questions assigned to the U.S. Commission on Obscenity and Pornography when that task force was created by an act of Congress in 1968. Two years later, after spending almost a million dollars on research, the commission concluded: "There is no reliable evidence indicating that exposure to sexually explicit materials leads to delinquent or criminal behavior."

Indeed, Dr. Cody Wilson, director of research for the commission, made the following statement in its ten-volume report:

> The results indicated that there is a relationship between experience with explicit sex material as an adolescent and later being a sex criminal, but the relationship is a negative one. The sex criminals reported less—considerably less—experience with explicit sexual materials as children and adolescents than did the normal men. This, of course, is contrary to popular rhetoric and myth, and we did not know whether to trust this finding or not. Luckily, four other groups of investigators were studying the same phenomenon for the commission, and the results of the studies were all consistent: sex criminals have less experience with explicit sexual materials in adolescence than do normal, non-sex criminal males.

In short, the commission's findings are that the emergence of adult bookstores and films which exploit sexual curiosity are symptoms of, rather than the cause of, the obsessional preoccupation with sex which exists in our society. It is the puritanical suppression of sexuality which has produced both the problem and the people who are easy prey to "sex-ploitation" in our culture. To further suppress the subject is, in Shakespeare's words, "to dismiss the physician and bestow the fee upon the foul disease!"

I would prefer to follow the commission's recommendation, which incidentally was ignored by the Congress, that we launch a nationwide, effective sex education program. There will, of course, be those who strenuously object to such an endeavor but, as the commission report put it, "Sexual information is so important and so necessary that, if people cannot obtain it openly and directly from legitimate sources and through accurate channels, they will seek it through whatever channels and sources are available."

The final, and for me crucial, consideration prompts the values clarification exercise cited earlier. On the one hand, I experience most sexually explicit films and picture books as vulgar, boring and offensive. They are obscene in the literal sense—that is, against life, because they portray persons as objects and I find that distasteful rather than erotic. I would prefer to live in a society where such debasements of human beings and sexuality did not exist. But, against that value of a culture free of such crude insensitivity, I must weigh a more compelling concern for the value of freedom. The right to decide for myself what I shall read or view takes precedence over my desire to be rid of X-rated movie theaters and adult bookstores in our community.

I believe that in a free society the government is never justified in censoring what a citizen may read or see unless and until it can be shown to be harmful. If we abandon that principle, we open the door to mind control. There's nothing to prevent a Mississippi jury from deciding that the television movie *Roots,* which contains two rape scenes, is pornographic, and from proceeding to prosecute the ABC network and author Alex Haley for bringing that kind of "filth" to their town.

Whenever I hear that some book should be censored, I remember the Gallup Poll figures indicating that seventy adults out of every one hundred in America don't read a single book in a year. It seems to me that the other thirty ought to be allowed to read whatever they please.

I regard the current wave of films which feature sado-masochism and brutality as shockingly distasteful, but it is the violence and the brutality exhibited toward women which offends me. Perhaps a case can be made for the harmful effects of viewing such violence on film and for censoring this modeling of brutality which is regularly seen in other films, as well as the "skin-flicks." We also get daily doses of such violence on our television screens, and if that can be demonstrated to be the cause of violent, criminal behavior, legal restrictions may be in order.

But I would move cautiously because, as offensive as violence is to me, to restrict our freedom of expression is worse than offensive. It is intolerable. We must find better ways of dealing with the matter.

Motherhood Ought
To Be a Choice

THERE IS NO SIGHT MORE IRRESISTIBLY charming than that of a healthy, smiling baby. Our nation's advertisers discovered that long ago. There is no relationship more revered than that between a loving mother and her child, and rightly so because that is where most children have their first experience of love.

Precisely because this is true, because the quality of the mother-child relationship is so important, there is nothing more tragic than the bearing of an unwanted baby. Each year thousands of battered infants are reported to the police, and for every one of them there are hundreds more whose lives are psychologically blighted by the abuse of parents unable to cope with their needs.

123

That is why I believe that motherhood ought to be a choice. That decision should be available to every woman—including those who have been unable to avoid pregnancy.

This, then, is a plea for the continued legalization of choice in the matter. It is not a denial of the significance of motherhood but a recognition of its importance. It arises from a desire to make motherhood always an occasion of joy and creativity.

In 1969, when abortions were illegal, I was one of the six ministers in Detroit who formed "The Clergy Counseling Service" for women dealing with unwanted pregnancies. Our purpose was simply to inform them of the alternatives available and, if they decided to terminate the pregnancy, to refer them to a qualified physician. After only a month of operation, the counseling service, comprising 67 clergy throughout the state, was handling 150 calls a week.

One of the persons I saw was a sixteen-year-old high school girl, accompanied by her parents. She was not ready for marriage. She could not take care of a child, and she could not cope with the trauma of giving up the baby for adoption. To insist that she must choose one of these alternatives seemed cruel and insensitive.

Another woman was the mother of five children, all under the age of seven. She and her husband pleaded that they could not care for the needs of the children they already had. Because the contraceptive pill made her ill, she had turned to other methods of birth control, and was now faced with the prospect of another child. The law which would have forced that consequence on that family seemed inhumane and unjust.

Then there was a divorced mother who had been on Aid to Dependent Children but, when her youngest child entered school, had gotten a job and experienced the dignity of being off the welfare rolls. Now she was pregnant. Should her indiscretion require that she have the child and go back on A.D.C.?

Should society punish her and her children because she transgressed a hardly-observed social code regarding extramarital sex? To do so would have been harsh, vindictive and shortsighted.

I could go on with hundreds of similar cases, all of which represent the desperate and sometimes suicidal circumstances which annually drove a million women to seek illegal and unsafe abortions. Many died in the effort. So, for humanitarian reasons, I support a woman's right to choose whether or not she will bear a child.

Another reason for retaining the option of abortion is a recognition of the civil liberties of women. It is their right to decide if and when they want to have a baby, and not the province of government to dictate such an important decision.

Margaret Sanger, the founder of Planned Parenthood, declared in 1920: "No woman can call herself free who does not own and control her own body. No woman can call herself free until she can choose consciously —whether she will, or will not, be a mother."

Let us now examine the primary argument against granting women the right to terminate a pregnancy: the contention that a fetus is a person and abortion is murder. The crucial question is: when does a fertilized ovum become a human being? Some contend that it is at the moment of conception, a stance which would brand as homicide some methods of birth control, as well as abortion. But for thousands of years most cultures allowed abortion on the assumption that "a fetus is not a person—until it has seen the light of day," as Judaism puts it. Indeed it is only recently, in certain Christian nations, that prohibitions against abortion have arisen. The common practice in Egyptian, Greek, Roman, and Far Eastern cultures was to allow abortions during the first five months of pregnancy.

For centuries Roman Catholic Christianity accepted the practice during the early months. The church had accepted Aristotle's contention that the soul entered the fetus on the fortieth day of embryonic development. That view prevailed until Aquinas articulated what was long the official view of Catholicism—that "ensoulment" accompanied "quickening," the woman's experience of the movement of life inside her at approximately four months, an idea which has some psychological significance. It wasn't until 1588 that Pope Sixtus declared all abortions to be murder. That decree was reversed by Pope Gregory three years later. Thereafter, the Catholic Church continued to permit pregnancy termination until Pope Pius IX declared again in 1869 that all abortions were murder.

I report this history to point out the irony of the church, which took so long to make up its own mind on the matter, wanting to decide it now for the rest of us.

That's the crux of the issue. I believe that embryonic development is a process, not a person. If those who think differently want to govern their lives accordingly, let them do so. No one will force them to practice abortion. But they have no right to impose their religious beliefs on all women. Abortion is not an ideal solution to a human problem; it is always a tragic, and terribly difficult, personal decision. However, in a republic that prides itself on the separation of Church and State, government has no right to dictate that decision and impose one religious view on the whole society.

Having taken that stance, I must say that I do so with a troubled heart. I regard reverence for life as the ultimate basis for all ethical decisions. Every other right derives from the fundamental right to live. It is, therefore, impossible to be ethically pure on this issue. There is no way to avoid compromise and arrive at a morally responsible position. An embryo, though not a person, is more than disposable tissue. It is a potential person and cannot be regarded casually without a deterioration of our sense of the sanctity of life.

However, I still believe in pro-choice because my reverence for life extends to all the other lives involved in such a decision. And I know that even Albert Schweitzer, who coined the phrase, recognized the occasional necessity of sacrificing one life to save another. But we should always do so with a heavy heart, lest we become insensitive and lose the very wellspring of religious feeling.

I hope the day will come when contraceptive techniques are so effective and the desire to use them so universal that this agonizing decision will not have to be made, when motherhood will always be an occasion for joy.

Gun Control is
Needed Now!

THERE IS A PSYCHOLOGICAL TEST FOR imbecility. The subject is placed before a tub being filled with running water and asked to empty the tub. If he begins to bail out the water without first turning off the faucet, he's judged to be abnormally stupid. I contend that it is stupid not to turn off the means by which most murder is done, while we look for ways to deal with the causes of violence in our society.

A few statistics will demonstrate that gun control is a matter of life and death in the United States. Currently more than 13,000 Americans are murdered annually by guns. Another 13,000 die by accidental and self-inflicted gunshot. That's seventy human beings a day, and twice as many per capita as any other nation in the world.

The comparative figures for handguns are even more dramatic. In 1983, handguns were used for the murder of six persons in Canada, eight in Great Britain, ten in Australia, twenty-seven in Switzerland, twenty-five in Japan, and 9,014 in the U.S. Add to that the suicides and accidental killings, and the total was more than 20,000 handgun deaths in the United States in that one year.

This rising rate of gunshot fatalities has resulted in the fact that, since 1900, there have been more deaths by firearms inside the United States than in all the wars our nation fought during that time.

Why does America continue to claim this dubious distinction of being the carnage capital of the world? The sheer availability of firearms is clearly a factor. There are more than 115 million privately owned guns in the United States. Forty million of them are handguns.

The logical solution to such a situation is, of course, to license and restrict gun ownership. The effectiveness of such measures has been demonstrated in other nations. In one year the 50 million people of Great Britain, where handguns are strictly controlled, had one-fourth as many handgun murders as the city of Houston, Texas. However, efforts to pass similar legislation in this country have been thwarted by a powerful lobby which calls itself the National Rifle Association.

The stated N.R.A. policy is "to resist any restrictive gun legislation at any level of government." It offers the following arguments which I think are more mythical than meaningful. The first is reflected in the bumper-sticker slogan: "Guns don't kill people; people kill people." That is a silly statement. The simple, obvious fact is that a person with a gun is more dangerous than someone without a gun, and "seven times more deadly than persons with all other weapons combined," according to the F.B.I.

Most murders are spontaneous acts, committed during the heat of violent passion. Without a handgun available, many of them would be turned into non-fatal assaults. It is idiotic to argue that a potential killer isn't more lethal with a gun. We might as well say bombs don't kill people, people do, and let bombs be stockpiled by every nut in the nation who can afford them.

The fact is that a handgun in the home is much more likely to result in death of a family member than of a burglar. Even with all the guns around, only two percent of burglars are shot each year. And for every one burglar who is stopped, six family members are shot in accidents. The best protection against law-breakers is not to arm everyone and thus turn our cities into shooting galleries, but to disarm the lawless.

The third myth is that of the so-called constitutional right to keep and bear arms. The fact is that the Second Amendment to the United States Constitution, from which that phrase is taken, states: "A well-regulated militia being necessary to the security of a free State, the right of the people to keep and bear arms shall not be infringed." The United States Supreme Court has ruled on four occasions that this does not guarantee the right to personal gun ownership—it merely establishes the right of the National Guard to bear arms for the protection of the State.

The N.R.A., however, insists upon presenting this as an issue of national defense, describing gun control laws as "a Communist plot to take over America" and suggesting that Russia is afraid to attack the United States "because they know that 30 million Americans own and know how to use firearms." They never explain how, after this fearsome invader has overwhelmed our navy with its battleships, our army with its tanks, and our air force with its nuclear bombs, it is going to be stopped by a citizens' rifle brigade.

Equally ludicrous is the N.R.A. paranoia about gun registrations: suggesting that the lists would be used by the Communists in their take-over as a means of finding such weapons and seizing them. It overlooks the fact that such information would be scattered in city records all over the country, and if the occupation forces really wanted such information, the best source would be the membership rolls of the N.R.A.

Underlying all the others, there is a more subtly pervasive myth suggested in an N.R.A. pamphlet which quotes its former president, Karl Frederick: "How contemptible, how degrading is the advice of those who tell us to submit meekly to the depredations of the bandit. Let them follow their counsels of cowardice if they prefer to surrender the privileges and the rights of manhood." There we get down to it: guns must be allowed, whatever the cost in human life, because they are a symbol of masculinity.

Thus the machismo myth rears its ugly head, and we see the Rambo mentality which equates manliness with a capacity for violence. This anxiety verges on being a national neurosis. It not only sustains our attachment to guns, but has pervaded our foreign policy for years, resulting in incidents like the Mayaguez fiasco where more men were lost than those who were rescued. The bravado with which the army, navy and marines—to prove their masculinity to the world—went after the tiny nation of Grenada was like someone after a mosquito with a cannon.

It's time we set aside such dangerous and destructive myths. When a man who had been arrested for carrying a loaded gun through an airport lobby, and who apparently had psychiatric problems, is able to go to a pawnshop, buy a handgun, and use it to attempt the murder of the president of the United States, it's time to enact some strong gun laws.

The Holy War—
Then and Now

WARFARE IS AS OLD AS HUMANITY.
Since the beginning of civilization, people have fought one
another for food, for land, and for natural resources, justifying
their aggression in terms of survival. But the most vicious wars
have been those fought in the name of religion. Sanctified
destruction seems to know no boundaries of decency.

The first manifestation of a holy war mentality was exhibited
by Christians and Moslems. It was called the Crusades and
lasted from the beginning of the seventh until the end of the
seventeenth centuries. Depicted in our history books as a
glorious adventure of noble knights, the Crusades were actually
a grisly business.

Setting out from France under the banner of the Cross, symbol of "The Prince of Peace," those supposedly righteous warriors began by beating Jews and burning their synagogues. Then they marched across Europe, plundering their way to Jerusalem. On July 15, 1099, they entered the Holy City, went to the Church of the Holy Sepulchre, knelt before the tomb of Jesus, and then proceeded systematically to slaughter every Moslem they could find. Men, women, children, old and young alike were killed until, according to their own accounts, the Via Dolorosa, where Jesus had borne the cross, was flowing with blood. The butchery was justified on the grounds that these people were unbelievers who desecrated the Holy Land with their presence. They represented the "anti-Christ" of Biblical prediction, which would rise up and destroy the world if it were not itself exterminated. The Crusades, later described by Pope Pius XII as "simply a difference between two forms of monotheism," continued for nearly 1,100 years, cost the lives of two million people, and finally stopped only when both sides realized that neither would prevail. They would have to learn to live together.

The next great religious war was fought among the Christians themselves. Again our history books tend to depict the Reformation as a polite theological debate, but it launched two hundred years of ruthless warfare. Catholics and Protestants mutilated, tortured, and murdered each other with a hatred that accompanies only a holy war view of the enemy as evil incarnate. The Roman Church saw Martin Luther as the anti-Christ, while Reformers viewed the Pope as fulfilling that role. Each side thought of itself as serving a sacred cause: the extermination of an irredeemable evil. Both finally fell back in exhaustion to recognize that they, too, would have to learn to live together.

By the eighteenth century many believed that we had seen

the last of religious wars. Conflicts continued, of course, but they were carried on by professional soldiers, armies which observed rules of civilized warfare. As one historian writes, "England and France were at war thirty-five minutes out of every hour during the 18th century, but there was no obsessive hatred of one people for another." In the midst of that kind of conflict it was still possible for one culture to admire the philosophy, literature, and art of the other. So in the nineteenth century, the holy war became regarded as a thing of the past. This belief, however, neglected the fact that religious fanaticism is capable of assuming many forms.

The cult of nationalism emerged. It has persisted and thrived. Today it is the reverent feeling of a national faith which evokes the deepest sense of belonging, commitment, and loyalty. It commands the strongest willingness to kill, if necessary, to protect the sacred honor of that political faith.

World War I was the first manifestation of this new kind of religious conflict. Ten million human beings were killed when supposedly civilized people—British, French, German, Italian, Austrian, Russian, and finally American—fell upon each other with a fury far out of proportion to the issues being disputed. Each was willing to believe the vilest stories about the other and to behave in ways that fulfilled their foes' fantasized fears. It is impossible to account for the intensity of the hatred exhibited, especially between the British and the Germans, whose monarchs were cousins, unless we recognize it as reflecting the fervor of a religious fanaticism, of which nationalism was simply the latest manifestation. A clear expression of the phenomenon can be seen in Nazism in Germany, where propaganda techniques were used so brilliantly to create a sense of divine destiny.

The next expression of the holy war mentality accompanied the emergence of the Communist ideology. Another example of secular religion, Communism had its sacred writings, its dogma and true believers, its evangelists and martyrs, and a characteristic intolerance of differing faiths of heretics within its own. The metaphysical base was atheistic, but psychologically, Communism, and the anti-Communism it usually engenders, bears the traits of religious fanaticism.

There are three facets of a holy war mentality. The first is that crusaders have always believed that theirs was a divine mission, that "God is on our side." The belt buckles of German soldiers said it explicitly: "Gott mit uns!" Communists would leave God out and talk instead of history being on their side, but the effect is the same—that of feeling self-righteously sanctified in their plunder.

With this mind-set, those who oppose you are seen as not merely your enemies but the enemies of everything that is holy. Anything you have to do, however immoral under ordinary circumstances, is justified by the righteousness of the cause— that of exterminating such satanic evil. A concomitant belief holds that any ally in that cause is automatically good, whatever immoralities he may be guilty of. Moral absolution is conferred as a reward for allegiance.

And so Christians slaughtered Moslems with holy zeal, and the Moslems, understandably, reciprocated. And when the savage Mongols, under Genghis Khan, swept out of Asia to attack the Islamic nations, the Pope received their emissaries as friends. They shared little else but a common enemy, but that was enough. And during World War II, when the Russians were fighting with the allied forces against Nazi fascism, they were "good guys"—but when that war was over they became the "Godless enemy," and instead of talking about "the Prussian military mentality," we began to refer to "the Slavic mind" as being "incapable of understanding any language but the language of force."

A second, related dimension of the Crusader mentality is the belief that the enemy is so diabolically evil that he is incapable of responding to a gesture of reason and goodwill. In psychological terms, our characterization of our foes as evil incarnate allows us to engage in projection—attributing to the enemy the basest impulses of our own nature. Indeed, some suggest that this is why we need "enemies."

Holy warriors fashion all kinds of fantasies and fasten them upon their foes. Christians saw Moslems as idolatrous, sexually licentious and inherently violent people, just as they themselves were viewed by the Moslems. Thus, too, have Catholics and Protestants, British and Germans, Communists and anti-Communists seen each other. In recent years some fundamentalist Christians have elevated all this into a pious parlor game of identifying the current enemy with "The Beast of the Apocalypse," the anti-Christ of Biblical prophecy.

This practice sets up the third element in the holy war mentality— that of seeing the enemy as such a powerful force of evil that, if we do not destroy them, they will destroy us. Since there is no co-existence with such monstrous bestiality, it is our sacred responsibility to eradicate it from the earth.

Christians and Moslems believed this of each other, but when Genghis Khan, of all people, finally persuaded them to sit down at a peace conference, they discovered, to their astonishment, that they had much more in common with each other than either did with the Mongols.

We won't have 1100 years to fight the next holy war. It could be over in eleven minutes, and almost everyone on this planet could die. The rest will wish they had. That is why it is important to recognize that there are those in our society, as there are in Russia, China, and other nations, who tend to generate the mentality of the holy war. These fomenters of a fanatical hatred must be identified for what they are, lest they stir up a frenzy of fear and distrust that could result in the destruction of our world. If you want to conjure up a deadly beast of apocalyptic dimensions, it is the holy war mentality itself which deserves that designation.

I am not suggesting that evil should be ignored; I applaud any effort to put morality into our foreign policy, to criticize and withhold financial aid from nations which violate basic human rights, especially if that policy were even-handedly applied. Nor am I proposing a unilateral disarmament, which would fail to recognize the realities of military might in our imperfect world. What I am warning against is the "hatriotism" of those who depict us as the divinely appointed guardians of truth and righteousness, with a holy calling to annihilate a so-called Godless enemy. It is that kind of paranoia I read in Alexander Solzhenitsyn's *Warning to the West,* with his words about our being "in the dragon's belly," another allusion to the Beast of the Apocalypse and a revival of the myth of Communism being a monolithic monster that threatens to devour us all. The fact is that modern Communism is no more monolithic than is capitalism. It is the kind of deliberate misrepresentation of the realities of our modern world which is always in danger of gaining popular acceptance, especially when people are feeling insecure and need scapegoats.

One of the first persons to recognize the futility as well as the immorality of the Crusades was Francis of Assisi. He asked his Christian contemporaries, "Do you not realize that Moslems also are human beings?" I suggest that we would do well to remember that Communists, too, are human beings, with no more innate capacity for evil than we have. Most people who live in Communist nations did not choose that philosophy of government, any more than we chose to be born in this country. But those who did, did so because they sincerely believed that it best served their personal and national interests.

Herblock, the political cartoonist, once depicted a global scene with a portly American looking across the ocean at a starving couple peering into a trash can for food. The trash can was labeled "Communism," and the caption below had the American saying, "How can they eat that stuff?" The answer, of course, is that they eat that stuff because they're hungry and there's nothing else to eat. The Cubans chose Communism because it promised them something better than they had known under the dictatorship of Batista. The Chinese chose Communism in preference to the oppression they experienced under Chiang Kai-shek. The Vietnamese chose Communism rather than economic exploitation by the French. And in each of these instances, our government had long supported the corrupt, oppressive rulers.

Those peoples' distrust of us is understandable. For our nation to view them now with paranoid hatred is a sign of weakness, not strength. It is more pointedly a projection of our own guilt. To say we must destroy them because of their political ideology is to trumpet our moral bankruptcy to the world. Most importantly, it is a prelude to cataclysmic conflict. Let us be done with such holy war mentality, lest it bring on the Armageddon we fear.

If Martin Luther King
Were Alive Today

W HAT WOULD MARTIN LUTHER KING
be saying and doing if he were alive today? I ask the question
because in recent years there has been a tendency to defame or
trivialize the man and his message in order to make him a more
manageable hero. School children are being taught that Dr.
King was a great orator who led the Montgomery bus boycott
and peaceful efforts to integrate Black people into our society.
And when the ceremony was held to proclaim his birthdate a
national holiday, it was the Marine Corps band, shortly after the
invasion of Grenada, that played "We Shall Overcome" while
the bust of this advocate of nonviolence was placed in the

141

Capitol rotunda. Not a word was spoken of King's passionate condemnations of militarism.

If we would bring fact to this fantasy, we must begin by overcoming what historian Vincent Harding aptly describes as "the massive, national amnesia concerning who that Black man really was." He goes on to say, "We Americans have chosen amnesia rather than continue King's painful, uncharted, and often disruptive struggle toward a more perfect union."

Let us recall some of King's words, not merely the graceful, poetic cadences of his oft-quoted "I have a dream" speech, but the more militant statements of his last few years.

In 1966 Dr. King voiced a commitment to all the downtrodden of this world when he said: "I choose to identify with the underprivileged. I choose to identify with the poor. I choose to give my life for the hungry."

As he sought to fulfill that commitment, however, he encountered the complex web of vested interests maintaining the status quo and was led to broaden the scope of his challenge. Addressing the Annual Convention of the Southern Christian Leadership Conference in 1967, he proclaimed, "The problem of racism, the problem of economic exploitation, and the problem of war are all tied together!" These were the "triple evils" that the freedom movement must address, he insisted, and seek nothing less than a "restructuring of the whole of American society."

His final public speech in Memphis on April 3, 1968, repeated the call "to make America what it ought to be," and expressed his long-held vision of the unique role of Black people in effecting the fulfillment of that dream. Only in the light of that magnificent obsession, that dual vision of achieving racial justice and thereby redeeming the soul of this nation, can we fully understand his more radical statements. Only as we remember the wholeness of King's vision can we appreciate his observation in 1967 that "Something is wrong with capitalism as it now stands in the United States."

And only as we grasp the full significance of that statement can we understand his saying, "We are not interested in being integrated into this value structure. A radical redistribution of economic and political power" is necessary to meet the needs of the poor in America.

When we recognize these dimensions of Dr. King's vision, we can better understand his condemnation of the American war in Vietnam. In spite of intense criticism from Washington and from the civil rights establishment, King spoke out, declaring at one point, "Never again will I be silent on an issue that is destroying the soul of our nation and destroying thousands of little children in Vietnam . . . The time has come for a real prophecy, and I'm willing to go that road."

So he prophetically exposed what he called "the paranoid anti-Communism which makes fighting mercenaries out of our jobless young men and sacrifices them to a militarism that threatens the future of the whole world." And though the current administration in Washington would like to pretend he never said them, perhaps his most compelling and still timely words were these: "A nation that continues, year after year, to spend more money on military defense than on programs of social uplift is approaching spiritual death!"

In his search for a more equitable distribution of wealth and power in America, in his determination to challenge our nation to "repent of her modern, economic imperialism," King did set out on a largely uncharted course. But having remembered the man as he really was, we can more accurately conjecture what he might be saying and doing if he were alive today.

You can be sure that he would be championing the plight of the homeless poor in America. He would begin by pointing out the staggering statistics which reveal the gaping holes in the

President's so-called "safety net" for the poor. Ten years ago in New York City there were 900 homeless families being given shelter by the city. Today there are more than 6,000 families being given a place to sleep, and thousands more on the streets. Those 6,000 families are being housed in hotels, one of which, The Martinique at Thirty-second and Broadway, houses 1,400 children, with an average age of six years.

The infant mortality rate at that hotel is twice the national average. Doctors call it "failure to thrive" when such "low birth weight children" die. And why the "low birth weights"? Because less than half of the mothers are eligible for food stamps, and those who are have had their food stamp allocations radically decreased in recent years. The allotment for a family of four went from $165 to $33 per month. And so children starve and government officials wring their hands and say welfare is bad for people; it discourages initiative and makes them lazy.

Dr. King spoke to that a long time ago, and his words are still true: "Whenever the government provides opportunities and privileges for white people, and rich people, they call it 'subsidies.' When they do it for the Negroes and poor people, they call it 'welfare.' The fact is that everybody in this country lives on welfare. Suburbia was built with federally subsidized credit, and the highways that take our white brothers out to the suburbs were built with federally subsidized money to the tune of ninety percent... The problem is that we all too often have socialism for the rich and rugged, free-enterprise capitalism for the poor."

Something *is* wrong with capitalism as it now stands in the United States. We continue to subsidize tobacco farmers, while allowing children to starve.

Dr. King might then point out these equally staggering statistics: for one trillion dollars you could build a $75,000 house, place it on $5,000 worth of land, furnish it with $10,000 worth of furniture, put a $10,000 car in the garage—and give all this to every family in Kansas, Missouri, Nebraska, Oklahoma, Colorado, and Iowa!

Having done that you would still have enough money left to build a $10 million library for each of 250 cities in that six-state region. And having done that you would still have enough money to build 500 schools at $10 million each for the region.

And having done all that, you would still have enough left of the trillion to put aside, at 10 percent annual interest, a sum of money that would pay the $25,000 a year salaries of 10,000 nurses and 10,000 teachers, not just for one year but forever!

That's how much money a trillion dollars is, the significance of which lies in the fact that, according to latest estimates, one trillion dollars is precisely what the Star Wars project would cost the American taxpayers.

If Martin Luther King were alive today, he would be thundering his outrage at such a preposterous misappropriation of our national resources, and leading a march on Washington to tell our elected officials that we will not tolerate such a paranoid allocation of our tax dollars.

Thirdly, in view of what he said about Vietnam, it is obvious that he would be similarly critical of our government's actions in Nicaragua. He'd probably describe it as another example of our nation's tendency toward economic imperialism: that the only freedom the Contras were fighting for was the freedom of American corporations to exploit the resources of that tiny nation without local interference—as we have for more than 100 years. If we really wanted to help the people of Nicaragua, he'd surely say, we would send them doctors and teachers and engineers, not guns and bombs. The best defense against the appeal of Communism is to help them create a more economically just society.

If we were truly concerned about human freedom, he might add, we would be exerting economic and political pressure on the blatantly oppressive government of South Africa. Our failure to act forthrightly in that situation, again because of economic interests, reveals the hypocrisy of our professed concern for human rights and proclaims our moral bankruptcy to the world.

And, finally, with much anguish in his heart, he would speak a chastening word to the government of Israel. Long a defender of that nation's right to exist in safety and security, he would, I think, express his dismay and sorrow at its violent repression of Palestinians in Gaza and the West Bank, the use of troops with live ammunition against unarmed, civilian demonstrators.

As he said so often and eloquently, hate begets hate, and hurt begets hurt, and violence breeds only more violence in this conflict-weary world. The only way the vicious circle is stopped is when people are able to set aside the "eye for an eye" mentality which pervades the Middle East, and strive to cultivate an awareness of our common humanity.

Faithful to the end of his martyred life to the principles of non-violent resistance, King would call us all to that difficult path of genuine peace-making.

Rabbi Abraham Heschel once introduced Dr. King to a Jewish audience with these words, "Martin Luther King is a voice, a vision, and a way. I call upon every Jew to harken to his voice, to share his vision, to follow in his way. The whole future of America will depend upon the impact and influence of Dr. King."

I think that's true. We must strive to keep alive in our hearts the courage that was in his, and preserve the impact and influence of his life. We, too, may be misunderstood, and maligned, and perhaps even martyred. But nothing less than our very souls are at stake, and the soul of this nation.

IN CLOSING

Shall We Pray

THE YEAR WAS 1880. THE PLACE, ENGLAND Seven women, soldiers in the Salvation Army, were being sent by boat as missionaries to the United States. Their commanding officer blessed them with the following prayer: "Lord, these ladies are going to America to preach the gospel. If they are fully given up to Thee, be with them, and bless them, and grant them success. But if they are not faithful, drown 'em, Lord, drown 'em."

A similar prayer was given by one John Ward, a member of Parliament who owned a good deal of property in England. "O, God, Thou knowest I have mine estate in the city of London and another in the county of Essex. I beseech Thee, God, to preserve the city of London and county of Essex from fire and earthquakes and, as I hold a mortgage in Hertfordshire, I beg of

Thee likewise to have an eye of compassion on that county too. As for the rest of the counties, God, Thou may doest with them as Thou thinkest best."

All of which illustrates why some of us have difficulty with the traditional practice of prayer. Historically it has been associated with the least attractive aspects of religion: primitive, superstitious, manipulative efforts to persuade a cosmic-errand-boy deity to give us what we want.

We also observe that the practice of prayer often acts as an opiate: dulling the ethical sensitivities of people. A woman once visited a church and apparently was much impressed with its liturgy, its elaborate ritual. On the way out she said to the minister, "I really enjoyed your lethargy." Too often, that's what prayer amounts to: lulling people into a laid-back mood which substitutes pious platitudes for social sensitivity. The obvious example of this is the fact that those who clamor for prayer in the public schools are the same persons who resist the racial integration of those schools. So, many of us adopt the attitude of Susan B. Anthony, who said, "I pray every single second of my life, not on my knees but with my work. Work and worship are one with me. I cannot imagine a God of the universe made happy by my getting down on my knees and calling him 'great.'" I agree, but I'm also inclined to agree with Thomas Carlyle who once wrote to a friend: "Prayer is, and remains, the native and deepest impulse in the human soul." When we examine that impulse, we discover that prayer can be of value—even to those of us who are wary of its distortions.

I believe that the native impulse and valid purpose of prayer is to move us toward the achievement of wholeness. Someone once said, "Prayer does not change things. Prayer changes people, and people change things." I believe that, and suggest that it operates at three levels. The first is internal: our relationship to ourselves. The second is external: our relationship with others. The third is all-encompassing: our relation-ship to life, to the animating power of being itself.

The goal in each of these relationships is wholeness. To the extent that we are divided within ourselves or estranged from others or alienated from life, we are not whole but broken. The purpose of prayer is to help us heal that brokenness.

But this endeavor requires that we acknowledge the fact that we are fragmented, and that is difficult. We are so busy trying to hold ourselves together that there is little time left, in any given day, to contemplate our brokenness. We also tend to avoid the effort because it is difficult. How much easier to run and hide, or simply keep muddling along until the sand runs out of the glass.

So the first thing prayer says is, "Stop. Catch your breath. Let the sediment settle in the muddy water of your life so you can see more clearly what is important." If you are too busy to spend a few minutes a day doing this, you are too busy.

There are many kinds of prayer, but they can be divided into three categories: those prayers that seek the healing of our brokenness, those which endeavor to reconcile us with one another, and those which represent an affirmation of "the burning one-ness of creation."

The first kind of prayer begins with confession, an acknowl-edgment of the fact that there are divisions within ourselves. You may be familiar with the litany: "We have done things we wish we had not done. We have left undone things we hoped to do. We have not lived up to the best that was in us." There is no human being alive who does not, at some time, carry such a burden. Robert Frost once confessed, "They cannot scare me with their empty spaces between the stars—on stars where no human race is. I have it in me so much nearer home to scare myself with my own desert places."

If we have not dealt with that reality, it *will* scare us. It will fill our present and shape our future. But if we face up to it, and commit ourselves to learning from it, we can make peace with our past and learn self-acceptance. That is the balm that heals. Confession is a pledge toward wholeness. It does not change the past. It does, however, help to bring the present out from the shadow of the past. And in this there is great power. Prayer does not change things, it changes people.

The next level of prayer is more complex. It encompasses petition and intercession. It has to do not with the past but with the future. It links not self to self, but self to others. At its most primitive level, it amounts to little more than begging. When it is selfish, there is no power in such prayer, but when it is caringly mindful of others, many good things begin to happen. We are taken outside of ourselves. Even the simplest of prayers, the child's bedtime petition, "God bless Mommy and God bless Daddy, Grandma and friends and pets and the trees, etc. . . ." cultivates connectedness. We become more sensitive to what we pray for, and it becomes a part of us. Our wholeness is enhanced.

Let me suggest a more difficult example. We are estranged from some person, and following Jesus' injunction that we love our enemies, we pray for them. I don't know why this is, but it's true: our attitude toward that person changes. And the way we behave toward that person changes as well.

To pray for another is to begin the act of reconciliation. Prayer can have an effect upon the future. It will certainly have an effect upon the present. We have little power over what others think of us, but we do have the power to free ourselves of envy and bitterness, of anger and hate—the things which fragment and diminish our lives.

To hold someone in our prayerful thoughts is to establish a bond, a connection that is holy and healthy and sustaining. Intercessory prayer may not physically heal another, but that person's knowledge of our concern can be a source of strength.

The deepest level of prayer comes in two forms which may seem contradictory, but are actually inextricably related. They are thanksgiving and surrender. Each is a way of saying yes to life. The former is a yes of gratitude. The latter is a yes of trust. Each is a way of blending dissonance into a larger harmony, a way of putting all of the disparate parts in the perspective of the whole. We ask nothing in such a prayer. We simply acknowledge the mystery and wisdom of the life process, the gift of being.

It is a way of letting go, and, if only for a moment, being swept away. Without demand, beyond regret, we yield and say yes to life. And there is grace and power in this. Past and future disappear. The present becomes one with eternity. All division, all brokenness, is overcome and we are whole.

I believe in the power of prayer. I believe in its power over the past that would control us. I believe in its power over the present that would elude us. And I believe that it is a healing power. It helps us to be less divided within ourselves. It helps us to be less estranged from one another. It helps us to be less alienated from the universe.

A story of prayer unexpectedly answered concerns a mystic who, every night after services in the synagogue would remain and, by the light of a single candle, sit and read the prayer book. At midnight he would seek a moment of communion, attempting to hear God's voice in answer to his own. One night he did hear God's voice, and the words were like music to his soul. "I have heard your prayer, my son," said the Almighty. "What is it that you wish? Ask and you shall be answered." "O Lord," the mystic sobbed, "I want nothing at all, except the bliss of Thy presence." God's reply was like thunder: "What! Is there no one you know who is hungry?"

Let us pray, and be prepared to be challenged and changed by the experience—toward wholeness.